Designs of Christian Baptism

BY

L. B. WILKES

"One having believed and having been baptized,
shall be saved."
Mark 16:16.

Charleston, AR
COBB PUBLISHING
2024

Published in the United States of America by:
Cobb Publishing
704 E. Main St.
Charleston, AR 72933
CobbPublishing.com
Editor@CobbPublishing.com

ISBN: 978-1-960858-67-2

Contents

Preface.

THERE is, in some minds, a prejudice against all writings that have about them the least bit of the spirit of controversy. In the preparation of the pages following it seemed to me to be impossible, at some points, to avoid the appearance of this evil.

It is admitted that the spirit of controversy is not most favorable to the discovery of truth, yet it is quite possible to have the appearance or form of the controversialist without possessing the spirit thereof. At least, I am conscious that, in the production of every sentence in this book, the work was done in an earnest, truth-loving, truth-seeking spirit, and with a prayerful anxiety to advance the cause of the great Master.

There are two enemies to the discovery of truth more to be feared than the spirit of controversy. They are ignorance and error. In any given effort to dispel one the other, the mode of procedure may not be the same as in some other similar cases. In *some* cases the soft sweet influence of thought and sentiment should come upon the heart of the hearer or reader like Aeolus' music, or like strains from Orpheus' lyre that are said to have aroused the interested attention of the dead in Hades. But in other cases, not a few, the style of "Jupiter Tonans" or of the actual cyclone would well represent the better mode of procedure. A wise general adopts the means and modes best suited to the case in hand as he sees things. So, one who would elicit or propagate truth, having of course to first remove ignorance and error, will adopt such means and modes of reaching his end as, to him, seem best. He may, of course, err in his judgment and do what he should not, or he may fail to do what he should.

The investigator should, In the first place, and as a matter of first importance, see that his own heart is right, not in his own eyes simply, but in the sight of God also. I have tried to keep this idea of primary importance constantly before me. How well I have succeeded the reader will decide for himself.

But if it be an evil to write in the spirit of a controversialist, as we have said, it is hardly a less frequent or a less dangerous one to write in a worldly spirit. It requires a brave, honest, sacrificing man to "agonize for the faith once delivered to the saints," but almost any sort of a so-called man can, by force of gravity, float with the current and try to please the world. This latter class—pleasers of men more than servants of God—is the one in which apostasies are begotten, in which "the man of sin" was born and nourished up into his present fatal power. So, let the man of controversy be censured, duly censured, if he must, but I fear more, much more, the one who is so sweet-spirited, so good, that he will controvert nothing.

If such a one should feel obliged, in any case, to enter a protest against any supposed error, the work is done so slowly, sweetly, mildly, so easygoing, that, like Caesar's river in Gaul, it is difficult to determine "whether he is going south or coming back." The road to truth is not always a smooth, flowery one. The traveler along that way is frequently compelled to make his way up rugged steeps and against painful obstructions.

The subject now before us is one that has been much discussed, and not always, nor even generally, in as amiable a spirit as it should have been. Indeed, there have been so many *controversies,* often angry ones, on the different phases of baptism, that the bare mention of the word raises, in many minds, feelings not quite pleasant. On this account I have found it difficult or impossible to so construct my sentences in some cases, as to feel sure that I was safe from the suspicion of being a controversialist, and of writing in his spirit. Moreover, I am so decidedly opposed to the goody-goody, sweet-spirited way of doing things that I may, unintentionally or inadvertently, have leaned too far the other way.

As it respects my manner of composition, I beg the reader's indulgence. I have written very plainly for plain people, that all might understand. But in respect to the positions I have taken and my reasonings thereon, I invite the most rigid, unsparing criticism, consistent with a high, courteous, Christian spirit.

I send this work forth to the public, fully aware of the fact that it will not be, in every respect, satisfactory to *everybody,* nor even to anybody. Indeed, the fact that its positions and reasonings are not in harmony with those of all others on the subject treated, is one principal reason for my having undertaken the work. Shall I be criticized, maybe severely? If I deserve it, as no doubt I do in some instances, I ought to be happy when it is well done; only let it be the "wound of a friend." If, in other cases, I do not deserve it, I shall not be hurt, but benefited rather thereby.

I have tried, as a brave soldier of Jesus ought, to be right, and not wrong in the production of these pages, and I pray my good brother who may read this book to be like-minded with me, that God may be glorified in and by both of us.

L. B. WILKES.
Stockton, Cal., Jan. 6, 1893.

Introduction

THough there have been many treatises on the different phases in which Christian baptism may be considered, in its so-called action or form, its subjects, its design, its administrator, its formulary, etc., yet if there has been, in a *separate volume,* a reasonably full and satisfactory effort made to set forth the teachings of the Holy Scriptures on the design or the designs of baptism, I am not aware of the fact. In the following pages I have attempted such a treatment of the subject as, to me, its importance seems to demand.

The power to reason is thought, by some, to be a characteristic of man. It is doubtful whether this is so. But, be this true or not, it is certain that it cannot be said of every one that he habitually employs this manly endowment. Let us hope that a goodly per cent of our readers will examine carefully the following pages; that they will, in the light of reason and revelation and in the fear of God, see whether these things be so or not.

The design of a thing is the reason of it; the necessity of a thing is the importance of it. To live is a design of eating, but eating is important (necessary) to living. Now, if a deed, or act, or a performance has no design, it is without reason, and, may be, against reason. He who requires or performs such an act is unreasonable, or he is something worse. Of course, Jesus Christ could not be the author of an appointment having no design.

When Jesus said: "Go ye, therefore, and make disciples of all the nations, baptizing them into the name of the Father and of the Son and of the Holy Spirit," there was, of course, some purpose or design in being baptized, some end to be reached, or some object to be attained. He who does not know what that purpose was, and now is, is without at least one good reason for doing it. But it does not, at all, follow that because one does not see the purpose for doing any given thing he must, therefore, fail of the blessings of it, on that account. Such one will, of course, lack the impelling force to do the thing required that there is in *seeing* the object of it, which is often a great loss. Indeed, it may be and sometimes proves to be, fatal.

One should eat to live, yet if he should eat only that he might live, or simply to gratify his appetite, though he should still live, yet he would fail of the pleasure and blessing that come of acting from a higher reason.

There are several reasons why one should be baptized who is a prepared subject for it. 1. One must, it is said, be baptized that he may be able to say he has obeyed the command that requires it. 2. One must be or may be baptized in order to be a member of the church, or that he may be in the kingdom of God. 3. One may be baptized that he may be in Jesus Christ. 4. One may be baptized in order to the remission of sins.

As Jesus did certainly order that certain characters shall be baptized, of course these characters must comply before they can say, truly, that they have obeyed this one of God's appointments. 2. No one is contemplated, in the word of God, as being a member of the church until or unless he is baptized. 3. Paul says we are baptized into Jesus Christ. 4. Peter says, we are baptized "for remission of sins." When we have reached "remission of sins," we have obeyed the command, "be baptized," we are in the church, we are "in Christ Jesus." Or, when we have been baptized we have obeyed this command, we are in the church, we are in Christ Jesus, we have remission of sins.

The reader is requested to note carefully and to bear in mind constantly that I do not hold, and that I do not attempt, in the following pages to prove that baptism has any virtue in itself to take away sins. God, *only,* has power on earth to forgive sins. Therefore, when I say: Baptism is for remission of sins, I do not mean that *it* does the forgiving, but that God forgives the sinner's sins in it; or, that God has put baptism, as a condition precedent, to the remission of sins.

The taking of food is certainly *a condition precedent* to growth and continued life, so that if one will not eat he shall die. Yet, no one should hold that food sustains life except as God is immanent in it for that purpose. So, baptism has no force or efficacy to remove sins except as it is an appointment of God, with God immanent in it.

If one should put baptism at its Scriptural value he would be much more apt to submit to it than if he should feel convinced that it is not at all important that he should be baptized. Convince him that baptism is non-essential, that he is just as sure of Heaven without it as with it, and he can manufacture excuses for not being baptized, or for procrastinating it, with great facility. This is true of good, very good, men. Indeed, such an one is not far wrong. One certainly need not be very particular about a matter if there is out little in it. If all men should believe in their hearts that if they should die unbaptized they would be forever lost, the, so called, mode of baptism would be decided correctly in a short time by them.

If one should believe with all the heart that his sins were already pardoned he would not be much concerned to be baptized. As he looks at the matter, his sins are pardoned and he has a clear title to a mansion in the skies; what more can he want?

But, says one, "it is a command of God, and one who is saved *will, must, wish* to obey all the commands of God. That is true. But, a command with no object or purpose is one without a reason; it is a *foolish* thing; and one is not apt to have a high opinion of the. need of doing anything when the necessity, which is always a reason of doing a thing, does not exist.

I do not say, for I do not believe, that a person must see that baptism is for remission of sins before it can be, to him, a valid baptism. God has not, in His Bible, said or intimated that when being baptized we must, in order to make the transaction valid, see or believe that we are doing so in order to be forgiven. He who is baptized in order to remission of sins as his purpose, in the sense and with the feeling that he is to get, therefore, (or rather *therefor,)* so much forgiveness, is a legalist. He can receive nothing of the Lord, unless it be condemnation. Such an one, in being baptized, is not serving the Lord, but *self,* rather.

But, to know what the blessings that come to the obedient are and to feel the mighty drawing, impelling force of them in bringing us to, and in keeping us in, the service of God, is a very different affair. All the drawing power there is in both heaven and hell is laid purposely before us to induce us to love righteousness and hate iniquity. Perhaps the highest reason that one can have for obeying any command of God is. that *it is God who calls for it.* If one sees that, in being baptized he is lovingly and in the exercise of an abounding faith, obeying his God, his Savior, but does not yet know the blessings in full that shall be his; does not know that the Lord has promised to remit his sins, to put him into Jesus Christ and make him a member of His church, he has, nevertheless, rendered obedience of the highest order; he has a valid baptism. He would be happier and stronger, and in many ways it would be better if he had known all the reasons why he should obey God in this, one of His appointments, before doing so. Still he is rightly baptized if he is conscious of but the one purpose in his heart, of obeying his Savior in love.

As pertinent, in this connection, I make a short quotation from A. Campbell on baptism, pages 147, 148:

> "The gospel system is a system of redemption—a deliverance of its subjects from ignorance, guilt, and bondage. It contemplates a new creation—a transformation

of man in body, soul, and spirit. It is, therefore, a great system of physical, moral, and spiritual means and ends. Hence, its doctrine, its precepts, and its promises are but developments of a remedial system, originating in the benevolence of God, guided by His wisdom and perfected by His power."

This scheme of mercy has its parts, and each of these parts has its own peculiar object. Faith is not a substitute for repentance, holiness, or righteousness; but a means to these ends. As a means, it is, indeed, indispensable to every one of them. Prayer, reading or hearing, and meditation are means of Sanctification. But any one of these, without the other, would be incomplete and incompetent to the end proposed. So of the positive institutions of the Christian System. Baptism, the Lord's Day, and the Holy Supper are indispensable provisions of remedial mercy. Not one of them can be dispensed with by anyone who desires the perfection of the Christian State and of the Christian Character. Eating, drinking, sleeping, exercising, though not of the same nor of equal importance, are, nevertheless, all essential to the preservation and comfortable enjoyment of the human system.

These things premised, we are induced, according to our plan, to institute an inquiry into the use of Christian baptism, or, rather, into the design of it. It is a conspicuous and prominent part of the Christian religion, and is spoken of and alluded to more than one hundred times in the New Testament. It is worthy of a full examination, and of the most respectful consideration and regard. It could not occupy so much space in so small a volume and yet be considered as a matter of indifference, or of but little importance. We must, therefore, regard it with the respect and reverence due to a very prominent divine institution.

But the *design* of this institution has long been thrown into the shade because of the wordy and impassioned controversy about what the *action* is, and who may be the proper *subjects* of it. Now, it must be confessed that whatever importance there may be in settling these questions, that importance is wholly to be appreciated by the *design* of the institution. This is the only value of it. The question concerning the value of any action is incomparably superior to the question, What is the act itself? or to the questions, Who may perform it? or, Upon whom may it be performed? We are, therefore, induced to believe that the question now before us is the all-important—indeed, the transcendent question, in this discussion.

The appeal, therefore, must be made to the proper tribunal. It must be carried up to the Apostles and Evangelists of Jesus Christ. What, then, do they propose as the design of New Testament baptism? We say *New Testament* baptism, because we have in that book 'THE BAPTISM OF JOHN," and the baptism ordained by Jesus Christ. Although not one, nor identical, they may materially unfold and illustrate each other. They both came from Heaven. They both immersed believing and penitent persons and were alike indicative of divine wisdom and benevolence.

The Harbinger was sent to prepare a people for the Lord. He designed to enlighten and purify them. Hence he was both a preacher of faith and reformation, and proclaimed 'the baptism of repentance *for the remission of sins.*' It would, then, appear from the very annunciation of John's baptism, that its design was of a transcendently important and interesting character." Thus wrote one of the greatest thinkers of this century.

Though it should be admitted that baptism is for remission of sins, the question might still be raised, In what sense is this true? He who understands what Sin is, and what it is to remit or pardon it, will readily see that in the original or causal sense nothing but a *person* can *commit* or *remit* a sin; and that no one can, in this original sense, remit a given sin except the one against whom the sin has been committed. In this original or primary sense, baptism is not, of course, for remission of sins; *it* does not remit sins.

It is not an interpretation or explanation of a Scripture that does not allow that a given Scripture is true. It is legitimate to enquire for the *sense* in which the language is to be taken. But a so-called explanation that *contradicts* the statement itself is vicious, is not allowable. For example, Mark says that John preached a baptism of repentance *for,* into or in order to, remission of sins. Any pretended explanation of this passage that says or signifies that John preached a baptism that was *not* for remission of sins, is to be, at once, rejected. Ananias said: "Arise and be baptized and wash away thy sins." Any explanation that teaches that Paul's sins were not to be washed away in his baptism is to be rejected at once, because it is not an *explanation* of the passage, but a *contradiction* of it. Peter says that "baptism now saves you." What should be thought of an attempt to show that this passage means that baptism *does not* "save you?" that is, to show that Peter did not tell the truth? But, as before stated, it is entirely proper to call in question the statement on the charge of wrong translation or to enquire for the *sense in* which the statement is or must be admitted to be true. This is our present enquiry.

In discussing the subject of causality good writers have considered the subject under the heads: "Original cause, meritorious cause, instrumental cause, concurrent cause, final cause," etc. These may or may not all be the very best terms to employ to express the ideas they are intended to convey. Still, almost any one knows that a given thing may be a cause of a result in one sense but not in another. To illustrate: An old wealthy man sees a person struggling in a swollen stream and near to drowning. He is too old and infirm to personally render the assistance needed to rescue the man. He offers $500 to anyone who will save the man. A brave young man present seizes a boat, and, at the risk of his life, pulls for the drowning man, whom he reaches barely in time to save him. The sinking man lays hold upon the means of deliverance and is saved. It may be said, truly, that the old man saved him, the young man saved him, the boat saved him, and that the man saved himself. If any one of these factors in the deliverance of the man had been lacking he would have perished. Each one of these factors, then, plays a necessary part in saving the drowning man, but each one is related to the saving in a sense a little different from that of any one of the others.

One may admire, especially, the unselfish interest manifested by the old man to save the life of a stranger. Another is more especially pleased with the conduct of the brave, dashing young man who, at the peril of his own life, saved the life of another. And still another might have his admiration and enthusiasm aroused more in contemplating the fine buoyant qualities and strength of the boat, which, though the water was so very rough and dangerous, out-rode its surging billows and brought its precious freight in safety to the shore. In giving an account of this matter each one of these parties would be likely to emphasize that feature of the whole affair that most affected him. If I were to say that the old man saved the drowning one, I would speak truly. If I should say the brave young man saved him, this, too, would be true. If I should point to a certain beautiful boat and say to a friend, that boat saved a man's life, it would be a truth, also. These designated persons and things all co-operated and concurred in saving the man's life; but each one saved him in a sense a little different from that in which any one of the others did, yet it is true that *each one saved.* It would, therefore, be right to say of each one of the persons and things mentioned, it was *for salvation.* The old man was *"for salvation* his money was *"for* salvation." The young man was *"for* salvation;" so were the boat, the oars and rowing, etc.

Does one say that God is under no such necessity or limitations as we are; that he is able to save *directly* without the intervention of any persons or things as conditions thereto? While it is doubtful whether this is true, with all the *probabilities* against it, still our enquiry is not as to what God *can do* in the matter of saving a soul from death, but rather what does he do and what does he require the sinner to do in order to be saved? It is certain that he has not revealed to us that he saves the sinner without the intervention of conditions to be complied with in order to salvation.

Though it is true, as before stated, that God, only, has power on earth to forgive sins, it is also true that even He *cannot save* the sinner unless he is in a condition ready for salvation. In order to this preparation the sinner must, is required to, fulfill some conditions, such as God has prescribed. This has always, in all dispensations, been the case, and shall be to the end. When the sinner is prepared for salvation, then it is God who proceeds directly to remit his sins. These preparatory acts and states are not Saviors. They are simply God-placed conditions on which He will, as he has promised, forgive. God *cannot,* be it said with reverence, forgive an impenitent, unbelieving sinner. Such a sinner must die, and God cannot prevent this result. Faith and repentance are *conditions* of the sinner's forgiveness, but they are not Saviors.

He who made the eye, can He not see? He who made the ear, can He not hear? He who made the heart, can He not understand? In brief, does not He who made man know best the conditions on which it is right and best to place His forgiveness? As He only does or can forgive, is it not almost intuitively certain that He only, till He shall reveal them, knows or can know the terms of the sinner's salvation? Therefore, our enquiry is not, what *can* God do or what ought He to do, in order to save from sin, but what does He require the sinner to do, on compliance with which, HE will save him.

In the Scriptures we are said to be saved, or justified, etc., by God, by Jesus, by the spirit, the word, the blood of Jesus, by faith, grace, hope, baptism, etc. Loyalty to God requires that we believe every one of these declarations of Holy Writ on the sole ground that it is the word of God. I am as much bound to believe that we are saved by grace as that we are saved by faith, and I am certainly bound to believe both or neither; for they both stand on the foundation of the Word of God. To deny both is infidelity. To believe one and deny the other is infidelity *and* inconsistency. This reasoning applies to all the things mentioned, by which we are said to be saved, justified, forgiven, etc.

Baptism is, by some persons, said to save as a symbol, or in a symbolic sense? I suppose that baptism is a symbol or is employed in a symbolic sense in the Scriptures. But we have no intimation in, nor evidence from, the divine teachings that it was *intended to symbolize the "remission of sins."* There is evidence that it was designed to symbolize the death, burial, and resurrection of Jesus and probably our own. See Rom. 6:4–12; I. Cor. 15:29, 30; and Col. 2:11–14, etc.

But I see no reason to suppose that God ever intended that it should symbolize the "forgiveness of sins." Of course I know that many modern speakers and writers have held that it does symbolize remission of sins. But no statement to the effect that the Bible teaches this tenet is of any force or value unless it be supported by a valid reference to the chapter and verse in the word of God, which reference I do not remember to have seen.

From the time of Tertullian, 190 to 220 A. D., there have been some misguided persons and parties who attached to the water of baptism a miraculous power in the saving of the sinner from sin. It was, at least early in the third century, thought that the

Holy Spirit entered into the water, and that when one was buried in it, in baptism, he received remission of sins and the gift of the Spirit. It was believed to possess talismanic or magical power to save, *in itself.* This absurd view was, early, carried to the extreme of holding that baptism has the power, in itself, of removing from one destitute of faith, heart, and will in the matter—an infant— the taint of, so called, original sin, the power of converting a lump of total depravity into a saint or an angel. This conclusion grew, largely and logically, out of a misconception as to the lesson of John 3:5. All parties, anciently, allowed that baptism was for remission of sins. So, when they read, ... "except one be born of water and spirit he cannot enter into the Kingdom of God," they supposed the passage applied to all persons; men, women, and children, infants, and idiots, etc. They supposed that infants were totally depraved and were liable to eternal damnation. They said, if this original taint is not removed, infants must be lost. They knew that baptism was for remission of sins, and they supposed that they could baptize the infant. But the infant could not believe, and even if it could be supposed to be a believer, the infant could not* make the confession with the mouth. What was to be done? No one, then, came to baptism without "confessing with the mouth the Lord Jesus." The infants could not do this. Well, as an expedient, I suppose, and as God had nowhere forbidden it, they determined to employ parties, who could talk, to answer the solemn question, for the child or infant. So, when it was asked: "Do you, A. B., believe with all your heart," etc., the sponsor spoke for the infant, saying: "I do." On this, the infant's confession, made by the God Father, it was immersed. The reasons for the infant's baptism, as they regarded the matter, were that it might be delivered from its sins, from the wrath of God and eternal damnation and be made a lively member of the church.

This theory and practice remain to this day with some religious parties. In some cases the theory is modified somewhat, whereas the practice of infant baptism is maintained. If those who introduced this view had seen or understood that God could not and did not make *a law for infants,* to which he bound them on pain of condemnation here and of damnation hereafter, they would have seen that the law of the Kingdom, as it is expressed in this verse, was made for those who were capable of understanding and of obeying it, and for none others. I repeat, this exaggerated, unscriptural view of the value of baptism grew out of the supposed evil consequences to infants of not being baptized. I refer to this question or subject of baptismal regeneration for the purpose, after getting it fairly before the reader, of saying that I do not believe that baptism is for remission of sins in such a sense.

The sense in which baptism is for remission of sins is that it is given by him who *only* has the right to speak on the subject, in the charter of our blessings and privileges as *a condition precedent to that* end. How that can be; or, whether that ought to be; or, may we not dispense with it and still obtain the blessings, are questions which I do not attempt to decide nor wish to decide. One altogether loyal to God, in his heart, does not ask him, nor does he specially wish to know, whether he cannot get to heaven without making an open confession before men; or, whether he may not be saved without joining the church, asserting that the church cannot save him; or, whether he cannot be saved without being baptized, etc. No, no; such is not the feeling or language of one deeply in love with God and His cause. The constant cry and aspiration of a loyal, loving heart is, "Lord, what wilt thou have me to do?" True, one may, without sin, enquire into these questions if he so desires. But one cannot do so *to see* how cheap the terms of salvation may be; but may do so if he wishes, only, to know what it is his duty to do. In making this enquiry one should, in great faithfulness, scrutinize the contents of his consciousness to see if there be the least leaning towards the side of wishing to obtain a bargain in the search. In other words, he should search to see that his soul is clean of every motive for believing and doing, other than that such is the will of God.

Be shy of expediencies. For though many expedients are right and necessary; though no church nor church work can be conducted far without adopting some things called expedients, still let the sign of danger be placed over that door-way. That is the door through which most danger comes to the cause. It is the way of the apostate. When the sheep leave the fold and go astray it is nearly always by this expediency-road. A few short steps taken, not absolutely necessary, prepare the way for more and longer ones. Especially should the young deal in expedients very sparingly.

A more solid, steady, grave, and intellectually "serious" love for God, and more careful loyalty to the word of God are, now, much needed in all directions.

"To the Law and the testimony," we make our appeal.

Section 1.
Baptism—Its Designs.

Chapter 1.
Some Preliminaries.

Baptism, as I shall speak of it in the following pages, is considered from the strictly Christian standpoint. I shall not treat at length of the Jewish washings, which were bathings of the whole body of unclean persons, in water, for ceremonial cleansing, and which are sometimes spoken of as baptisms. These will, however, be noticed to a very limited extent, further, as we proceed.

It is not my purpose to discuss what is sometimes termed classic baptism. Classic baptism had no design; that is, no *one specific* design. It was not an ordinance of an institution with a specific function in said institution. Classic baptisms were merely facts in history. They were sometimes accidental, sometimes merely natural events; sometimes they were the doings of men, though often, they were not. In many cases they were without any design; in some cases their design was one thing, again it was another. In many cases the baptism involved, directly, the whole of the object baptized; in some cases it reached only a part of the object baptized, in which cases the baptized part is always mentioned. Nor do I intend to treat of John's baptism, except as it was a forerunner of Christian baptism, and, incidentally, throws much light on it. It was through John's baptism as one of the means that Christ was manifested to Israel as the Son of God; and it was also, "for remission of sins." Though I shall refer to these things and discuss some features of them to a limited extent, the *design* of Christian baptism is my special theme.

It is a fact that Christ instituted the Christian religion, that it, looked at as a whole, has a Gospel which Jesus required, and now requires, his disciples to preach, and connected with which as parts of a whole are baptism, etc.

Baptism was, no doubt, put. into the remedial system for a

reason or reasons. Indeed, it has, plainly taught in the Bible, two designs, one as a mere ordinance, or as a condition in order to a specified end. In this case it is for remission of sins. Besides this it has a design as a symbol. As a symbol it does and it was intended to declare a *burial* and a *resurrection.* As a mere ordinance or condition, any other outward and formal thing would have served the purpose as well as the thing selected. As a teaching or declaratory symbol, nothing else than baptism would have been so efficient.

It is in the nature of things necessary that, in uniting with any institution or organization, conviction that it is right, necessary, duty, or desirable, for some reason, or on some account, to do so, is required. It is not possible for the union to take place without it; nor can *any* one step or more be made in the direction of such union until it is a fact. Then this conviction must go to the heart and effect repentance, or a *resolution* to change. After both these, and in addition to them, there must be some overt, formal act, of accepting or embracing the thing proposed. This is seen in the case of marriage, naturalization, Odd Fellowship, Masonry— everything. All this grows out of the nature or necessity of things; or, which is the same thing, it is of the nature of God and man that it must be so.

In constructing the Christian System, therefore, it must needs have been that the sinner should be required to believe and repent; and then, as he takes upon himself new relations and obligations, he must have some formal way of doing it. There must be a turning act. It may be of any form agreeable to the law-giver in the case; or, looked at as merely a condition or turning ordinance, it need have no particular form. Any one public or overt act is as good as any other.

On the Pentecost the order was, "Repent and be baptized," and remission of sins followed.

In the next chapter, by the same speaker, guided by the same spirit of truth, the order of events is, "Repent and turn," in which case *turn,* or the act of turning is clearly the act of being baptized. Baptism is the turning act, required by the Lord, of the sinner, in renouncing the service of the wicked one and espousing the cause of Jesus Christ. Faith and repentance prepare the sinner for the turning act. There can be no such thing as the turning contemplated in becoming a Christian without these two qualifications precedent to any attempt or pretense at turning.

The Bible says of those who believe and are baptized, they shall be saved, or their sins shall be pardoned. It also says, of those who have believed, that if they shall "repent and be baptized" their sins shall be remitted. Baptism is, then, an ordinance for remission of sins. This is one of its designs. Of course it is not ourselves nor the ordinance that does the remitting. God does this, but He does it on His own terms. Now, that *we* might know that He has done it, and when He did it, He has said that if we should, being already qualified in head and heart, be baptized or turn to God, He would forgive us. We see, then, that in the nature of the case, and as shown in many plain passages of scripture, baptism is for remission of sins.

But, God meant to do and did do more, in designating a turning ordinance or act, than simply to assure the sinner of the condition and thus of the fact of his forgiveness. He meant to do more through this ceremony of espousiug the sinner to Christ than merely to announce that the ordinance is for remission of sins.

God made it a *teaching* ordinance, a symbol of the prime facts of the gospel. Paul says that the gospel, as it respects its elements of power to turn men, is, "How that Christ died for our sins, according to the scriptures, and that he was buried, and that he rose again the third day, according to the scriptures." These are naturally and scripturally, elements of the greatest power for moral and spiritual turning that it is possible for the mind to conceive. The ordinances of the Christian System—the Lord's Day, the Lord's Supper, and the Lord's Baptism—gather about these potential facts of the gospel as bees do about their queen, or as the true heart does about its real idol. The Lord's Day, or first day, says, Resurrection. Its history, taken in connection with the event it celebrates, is a power in establishing the resurrection of Jesus Christ. He who does, in any way, interfere with the testifying of this witness that it shall not bear its testimony to Christ's resurrection is no friend of God or man.

The Lord's Supper speaks, and has been speaking, for eighteen hundred years, saying: "He died for our sins." What a power to soften a heart, to turn a rebellious spirit to God there is in the, believed, announcement that "Christ died for our sins."

That we may see the direct testimony to our Savior and to the potential facts in his life and death borne by baptism, I invite attention to I. John 5:5–10:

> "And who is he that overcometh the world, but he that believeth that Jesus is the Son of God? This is he that came by water and blood, *even* Jesus Christ; not with the water only, but with the water and with the blood. And it is the Spirit that beareth witness, because the Spirit is the truth. For there are three who bear witness, the Spirit, and the water, and the blood: and the three agree in one. If we receive the witness of men, the witness of God is greater: for the witness of God is this, that he hath borne witness concerning his Son. He that believeth on the Son of God hath the witness in him: he that believeth not God hath made him a liar; because he hath not believed in the witness that God hath borne concerning his Son."

The fact or truth testified to is herein seen to be: Jesus Is the

Son of God. To establish this proposition, there are three that bear witness, "the Spirit, and the water, and the blood; and the three agree in one." Herein we see the thing to be proved, and these are the witnesses which John brings forward. These witnesses, I suppose, are the *truth,* or the Bible, for, "the Spirit is the truth;" baptism, for water is present nowhere else than in baptism; and the Lord's Supper, for it is said, "This is my body;" "This is my blood." The apostle does not say that these witnesses did testify at some past time and stop, but he says they are now testifying. That baptism did and was meant to testify to the Sonship of Jesus, is further shown by the fact that John the Baptist's baptizing was for the purpose, one leading purpose, of manifesting Christ to Israel as the Son of God. "I have also seen, and have borne witness that this is the Son of God."

"On the morrow he seeth Jesus coming unto him, and saith, Behold, the Lamb of God, which taketh away the sin of the world! This is he of whom I said, After me cometh a man which is become before me: for he was before me. And I knew him not; but that he should be made manifest to Israel, for this cause came I baptizing with water. And John bare witness, saying, I have beheld the Spirit descending as a dove out of heaven; and it abode upon him. And I knew him not; but he that sent me to baptize with water, he said unto me, Upon whomsoever thou shalt see the Spirit descending, and abiding upon him, the same is he that baptizeth with the Holy Spirit. And I have seen, and have borne witness that this is the Son of God."

This is the institution in which Jesus was recognized as the Son of God by his and our Father, who is in Heaven. It is here we meet with the spirit of adoption whereby we cry, Abba—Father.

What does baptism say on the question of Jesus' Sonship, and how does it say it? Paul says: "Jesus was declared to be the

Son of God by the resurrection from the dead." That is, the resurrection proved, established the Sonship. So, if baptism testifies to the fact of the resurrection, which it does, it, then, testifies to the Sonship of Jesus.

Baptism is a symbol, not a sign. A sign is never *like* the thing signified. A symbol is always, in some marked respect, a resemblance of the thing symbolized. A small human track seen in the sand is a sign that a child has been there; a cloud is a sign of rain; certain features are a sign of a knave. But the track is not *like* the child; the cloud is not *like* the rain; the features are not *like* the knave.

The lion is a symbol of strength; so, if a man should have great power among men we say he is a lion. Jesus was called a lion because, in respect to strength, he is like a lion. In respect to meekness, he is called, symbolically, a lamb. The evergreen is a symbol of eternal life, because it does not seem to die.

Baptism is not put into the scheme of salvation as a sign of anything; but in it we "were buried," and in it we were raised up, like Jesus was, or in a likeness to his resurrection. Rom. 6:4–5. We are also said to be "united together in the likeness of his death," in our baptism. In it we enact a burial and a resurrection. It, then, clearly symbolizes the burial and resurrection of Jesus, and was meant to do so. Now, as it is seen that God designed to have, in the monumental ordinance that should be the formal acceptance of the gospel, a striking symbol of two out of three of the chapters of the gospel, it is plain that a burial in water and a resurrection out of it was the thing to select, and that nothing **else** would have been so appropriate. Hence, baptism testifies, in regard to the Sonship of Jesus, a *burial* and a *resurrection.* This, as a symbol, is its language, its testimony. Paul says, in effect, that, in demonstrating the resurrection, the Sonship is shown or declared. The apostle John says it testifies to the Sonship of Jesus, and John the Baptist testifies that by or through it Jesus was manifested to Israel as the Son of God; and I. John 5:5 says the belief of this truth, most gracious and grand, is the victory over the world.

Baptism is, then, an important witness to the most important proposition in the world. The interests involved in the proposition—Jesus is the Son of God—are no less than *eternal life and death.* This witness ought certainly to be allowed to testify unembarrassed and untampered with. It, certainly, ought not to have its tongue taken out, so that it cannot talk. When it is seen, and wherever it is seen, it ought to be seen as a witness on the stand testifying the burial and resurrection of Jesus, and by implication, announcing our death. In baptism, the things symbolized are burial and resurrection. The power of the symbol as a witness, and the ground of its having been selected as such, are in its adaptedness to set forth these two gospel chapters. Take away the form, or the exhibition of a burial and a resurrection, from a baptism, *if that could be,* and the life is gone from the symbol and it speaks no word for Jesus anymore. I have thus, as a preliminary to the main theme, said, if I have not shown, that this ordinance has two designs; in the first place, "it is for remission of sins;" in the second place, "it symbolizes the burial and resurrection of Jesus Christ, and, by implication, it announces that he died for our sins."

It is said in some of our papers which advocate certain tenets of religion, and also in some of the symbols of faith, that "baptism is an outward sign of an inward grace;" or that it is a "Sign and Seal" of something. But baptism is not a *Sign* or *Seal* of anything, except as it is set down in the scriptures, or as it is fixed upon by Divine authority as an evidence or proof that the Sign—baptism—being present and seen, the thing signified—remission of sins—may be inferred. Signs are conventional agreements or natural suggestions to the effect that, when employed, certain things may be inferred. Or, signs are, sometimes *authoritative statements,* such that, when the thing, designated as a sign, is seen, the thing designated as signified, must, on the authority of the appointor, be inferred. So, baptism is, in a sense, a sign that one's sins are, have been, or shall be remitted, if Divine authority has so appointed, but not otherwise. So, admitting that baptism may be a sign of remission of sins, the question whether it is a condition of remission, is an open one. What its precise relation to the remission of sins is, is a point that must still be determined by the Word of God. To do this is our purpose in the following pages.

Chapter 2.
Baptism is for Remission of Sins.

THE plan proposed for the investigation of this question is the following:

1. The meaning of the terms.

2. The meaning of the proposition.

3. What is not meant by it.

4. Some objections to it answered.

5. Is the proposition true; that is, is the subject so related to the predicate that the latter must be affirmed of the former and not denied.

1. Meaning of the terms.

(a) The first term in the proposition is the word Baptism. This is the name of a duty enjoined in the New Testament by Jesus Christ by the employment of the word which names it. When Jesus commanded his disciples to baptize, what did he intend them to do? The word which he employed is *baptizo* in some of its forms.

When the Savior said: "Go, teach all nations, baptizing them," etc., that is, when he instituted the ordinance called "Christian Baptism," he had before him a number of words, any one of which he might have selected, and *a certain one* of which he would have selected in the use of which to designate the thing he wished them to do according as he meant them to do one or another thing. The word *mpto* was before him, which is used seventeen times in the New Testament. It is, properly, rendered *wash* in the common version, in every case, as the hands or feet, etc. It is never employed to designate baptism. *Louo* is found six times, employed by the Holy Spirit, but never in reference to baptism. It is translated *wash* in every case, and is applied particularly to the washing of the body.

Raino or *Rantizo* is used four times in the New Testament, and is rendered, properly, sprinkle in each case. It is never applied to baptism. *Cheo* does not occur, alone, in the New Testament. It is found with the prepositions, *kata,* twice; *epi,* once; and *ek,* eighteen times. It is never used in connection with the ordinance. It signifies to pour. If, in enjoining the duty of baptism, He had intended any one of the things above named to be done, he would have employed the word for it. Or, as he did not, in any case, use any one of the foregoing words in connection with the ordinance of baptism, it would seem that he did not intend any one of the things signified by any one of these words to be done in the matter of being baptized. If this conclusion be not correct, I see not why it is not.

Brecho occurs seven times, and, in the common version, is rendered *to rain* five times, and *to wash* twice. It means to *"wet, moisten, water,"* etc. If Jesus had desired any such thing to be done as is seen in the definitions of this word, this would have been the word to use. It is never applied to the ordinance. If *brecho* had been selected as the word to point out the duty of being baptized, it seems to me we would have been allowed to choose for ourselves any one of very many modes. This would have been liberal and agreeable to the tastes of sin-loving people. But, as before said, this word was not selected.

"Go, teach all nations, baptizing them," is the language of Jesus, "Repent and be baptized," is the language of Peter. In the former quotation the apostles are commanded to do something called "baptizing them." In the latter, others than the apostles are commanded to suffer or submit to something called baptism. Now, what is that thing which the apostles were to do and certain others were to have done? Evidently the Savior and Peter expected those whom they addressed to understand them. This, however, they could not have done unless the words they used had a current meaning at the time, and were employed by them in that current sense. This is so obviously correct, that, to demonstrate, illustrate, or elabor ate it, is wholly unnecessary. It is conceded by all intelligent, thinking men.

It is, then, assumed as undeniable that the word *baptizo* had, in the lips of Jesus and the apostles, a current and well understood meaning. It is further assumed as a proposition not to be questioned, that, in giving a revelation to man for the salvation of his soul, the Lord did actually employ the word *baptizo* in its usual current signification, unless he gave notice of a different sense. And since it is a fact that there is no intimation in the scriptures of a sense being given to the word different from the usual one, it was, beyond doubt, so used. We are left, then, with a necessity upon us of understanding this word, as all other words in the scriptures, in its ordinary sense. What, then, was the current meaning of this word, the first term in our proposition, at the time the Savior and the apostles employed it? This we must learn from its history. We may gain a knowledge of the history of it by actually examining the history for ourselves, or we may enquire of those who have made the examination. The result of the enquiry or examination is that *all scholars, critics, lexicographers, commentators,* and *church historians, are agreed as to this;* all, I mean, who are *authority,* and who have spoken on the subject, that it signifies to immerse. Dark shadows and harassing doubts, which will gather and thicken as we near the judgment, hang over and about every other practice for baptism than immersion.

There is a blissful certainty in this. I cite the testimony of *only a few* impartial, distinguished scholars as witnesses in this case, since it is not my purpose to discuss the topic to any considerable length.

Moses Stuart says: *"Bapto* and *baptizo* mean *to dip, plunge, or immerge* into anything liquid. All lexicographers and critics of any note are agreed in this."* When *such a man as Mr. Stuart was,* who practiced sprinkling or pouring for baptism, gives such testimony as herein, it about settles the question. In it, as he says, we have the testimony of *all lexicographers and critics.* Again, Mr. Stuart says: "But enough. 'It is,' says Augusti (Denkw. VII., p. 216), 'a thing made out, viz., the ancient practice of immersion. So, indeed, all the writers who have thoroughly investigated this subject conclude. I know of no usage of ancient times which seems more clearly made out. I cannot see how it is possible for any candid man, who examines the subject, to deny this.'"

Prof. Charles Anthon, of Columbia College, N. Y., says:

> "The primary meaning of the word, ('baptizo') is to dip or immerse, and its secondary meaning, *if ever it had any,* all refer, in some way or other, to the same leading idea. Sprinkling, etc., are entirely out of the question.
>
> "Charles Anthon."
> (Signed) March 27, 1843.

When Charles Anthon made that statement to us we received the same thing in it as if the name of every scholar and critic in America had been subscribed to it.

Prof. E. A. Saphocle's lexicon of the Greek language, current from 146 years before Christ to 1100 years after Christ, says: *Baptizo, to dip, to immerse, to sink.* Of *Baptismos,* he says: *A plunging, immersion. Bapto, to dip. 2. To dye. 3. To baptize. 4. To phlngc* a knife. The idea of anything but immersion as a meaning of the term baptize is wholly absent from the lexicon of this distinguished Greek author.

Dr. Philip Schaff, lately called to the chair of Church History in Union Theological Seminary, and late chairman of the American Committee on the New Version of the Scriptures, says:

> "On strictly exegetical and historical grounds baptism *must be immersion.* Without prejudice no other interpretation would have been given to Bible baptism. It is the most natural interpretation, and such we must always give. Immersion is natural and historical; sprinkling is artificial and an expedient for convenience sake. All the symbolism of the text, Rom. 6:3–4, and everywhere in the Bible demands the going under water and coming up out of it to newness of life. Sprinkling has no suggestion of burial to sin and resurrection to holiness. In order to be true to its original meaning and its vital relation to redemption through Jesus Christ, baptism must be immersion. Why do you wish to get rid of it? Eminent theologians have wasted their learning attempting to defend infant sprinkling. *Imposition is not exposition.* All the early defenders of Christianity taught that nothing but immersion was baptism, and all the Greek or Oriental churches continue to immerse to this day."

Dean Stanley, of the English Church, says:

> "What, then, was baptism in the apostolic age? In that early age the scene of the transaction was either some deep wayside spring or well, as for the Ethiopian, or some rushing river, as the Jordan, or some vast reservoir, as at Jericho or Jerusalem, whither, as in the baths of Caracalla at Rome, the whole population resorted for swimming or washing. The water in those Eastern regions, so doubly significant of all that was pure and refreshing, closed over the heads of the converts, and they rose into the light of heaven, new and altered beings." "For the first thirteen centuries the almost universal practice of baptism was that which we read in the New Testament, and which is the very meaning of the word 'baptize '—

that those who were baptized were plunged, submerged, immersed into the water."—*C. Q. Review,* Dr. E. W. Herndon, Jan., 1886.

Lyman Coleman says: "The baptism of John was by immersion."—*Ancient Christianity Exemplified,* p. 365.

Mosheim, in his *Church History,* says: "In this century (the first) baptism was administered in convenient places without the public assemblies, and by immersing the candidates wholly in water." As to the baptisms of the second century, he says: "The candidates for it were immersed wholly in water," etc.

Neander, Vol. I., p. 310, says:

> "In respect to the form of baptism, it was in conformity with the original institution and the original import of the symbol, performed by immersion," etc.

To these, add the testimony of nearly every *scholar* who has spoken on this question, in every century since Jesus said, "Go, teach all the nations, baptizing them," which all is to the same effect, and the conclusion is, the first term—baptism—of our subject is immersion.

These specific citations from witnesses certainly not prejudiced in favor of immersion (and the number might be increased by hundreds) are sufficient for my present purpose.

(b) Sin is the term which comes before us next, in logical order. What is its meaning? I. John 3:4, says: "Sin is the transgression of law," or, sin is lawlessness. And again, I. John 5; 17: "All unrighteousness is sin." These two statements furnish us an exhaustive definition of sin. Whatever is either of these is sin; whatever is neither of these is not sin. Of course, no one not responsible for a knowledge of law and obedience to it, can be a sinner.

Now, though the foregoing, as a mere definition of sin, must be allowed to be perfect, yet, he who knows no more than simply to repeat the words of the definition, knows but little of sin.

Sin is to be really learned from its history, as a tree is to be known by its fruit. Go to the whiskey saloon just after a murderous fight among the insane ones who gather, daily, at such places to curse God and their own souls. See the dead lying around; listen to the groans of the dying and to the shrieks and wails of widows and poor, ragged, fatherless children, and learn what sin is. The veil might be lifted from many a sadder, awfuler scene than this even, where countless millions are literally cursing the day that gave them birth, and this everywhere, every day, and every hour of this *weary, weary* life, and yet the half not be told.

No attempt of tongue or pen of mortal man can make sin appear as sinful as it is. The coming preacher of this generation is not the *young, delicate, handsome, drawing mistake* that an ungodly, unregenerate membership too often looks for, longs for, yearns for, and is almost insanely bent on having, but he is the one who knows and dares to stand up before the sinner and reason of righteousness, temperance, and the judgment to come, *so that the sinner is made to tremble,* and is made to cry out: "Lord, what wilt thou have me to do?" What the world that is under the power of the wicked one needs in the matter of preachers is not such as shall please the world, so much as such as shall be able to speak of sin, righteousness and the judgment according to the will of God.

The word sin is not used herein in its strict sense, as above defined. It is employed to designate, not what sin is so much as what its effects are, or what its consequences must be upon the soul that sins. Thus, the soul that sins is *guilty* and is *liable to be punished.* I employ the word sin then to signify, not what sin, strictly speaking, is, but to signify a state of *guilt,* and consequent *liability to punishment.* This brings us to the consideration of another term in our subject—remission.

(c) Remission is a sending away. When God remits sin he

sends it away so that it troubles the sinner no more. God removes the sense of guilt and all fear of punishment, and thus are we said to have remission of sins. This act of remitting sins has been thought to take place within the soul of man; to be a sensible act coming within the range of the consciousness of the pardoned one. The forgiven one is sometimes supposed to *feel* the act of forgiveness at the moment of its occurrence, and to be able, by some means, to recognize it *as* the act of God in forgiving his sins. This is, of course, a very erroneous, foolish notion, wholly destitute of any support from reason or revelation. The act of pardon is an executive one. It takes place in heaven, not in us; in the mind of God, not in our hearts. God only, in the first instance, can know that the act of pardon, in any case, has taken place, just as the executive of a State is the first, and, till he chooses to declare it, the only one who knows that a convict is pardoned. The knowledge of the fact of pardon in the case of one who sins against his God, and of one who sins against the law of his country, is in each case alike, a matter of faith, not of feeling. This faith is, of course, dependent upon testimony. The testimony must, in the nature of the case, come from God. He might declare to the sinner personally, "Thy sins are forgiven thee;" or He might ordain a law of life, upon compliance with which he would pledge the forgiveness of the sinner. The sinner being assured of pardon in either way viould have simply the word of God upon which to lean and trust that all is well. More than His word, God could not give us.

The mode in which God communicates to the sinner the knowledge of forgiveness is not to be assumed; it must be proved. The proof must be found in the word of God. If it be asserted that God speaks directly to each sinner pardoned, and declares to him the fact, that must be proved. The evidence that it is God who speaks, and that what He says is proof of the proposition to be proved, must also be clear. But God does not speak directly to the sinner, saying in audible language, thy sins are forgiven thee. Of course He does not. Does God convey to the sinner assurance of His pardon by giving to him a "feeling sense of the fact?" Waiving the question of the *possibility* of God's giving the assurance in question, in this way for the present, is it true that he does?

Suppose a sinner is conscious, at a given time, of a feeling, either good or bad, may he conclude, hence, that his sins are pardoned? We are conscious of a very great variety of feelings, both pleasing and painful, and of an almost infinite number of different degrees of the same feeling, during our lives. Does God's word declare that any one of these feelings, or any degree of any one of them is His voice in us proclaiming our sins forgiven? Moreover, how could we identify the feeling which, at any time, we might have as the one which is to be accepted as the proof feeling of our proposition? and how could we distinguish it from the other thousands of consciousnesses which we daily have? Has God said *the* proof consciousness is one of a *pleasing character?* He, in his word, certainly does not say so. But, admitting that He does, how pleasing must it be before it is to be taken as proof? Shall we say that it is the most pleasing experience of our life? that when such an experience is had it is to be accepted as proof, and that we are thereby assured that our sins are forgiven? If this were the criterion governing in the case, no one could be sure that he is pardoned till his life ends. The satisfaction of being sure that God has accepted him, could never, during life, be his; for, till death, he does not know but that an experience, more joyous than any previous one, might occur.

But this theory involves a plain contradiction of the word of Goa. The scriptures teach that some persons, at least, will not be saved. Whereas, according to this hypothesis, *all* must be saved; for there is not an accountable human being in the world and never has been who has not had or will not, at some future time, have an experience, the happiest of his whole life.

It is, also, certain that, admitting it to be possible to give to the sinner, in his consciousness, proof of his pardon, it would be necessary that he should have that particular impression which should be to him the proof of his acceptance with God, most unmistakably distinguished from all others; and this distinction *God* must make, else there is no proof in it. True, if God should work a veritable miracle in attestation, and the sinner could know it to be such, of course the proof would be satisfactory; for in that case he would have the proof which I have herein demanded. I, then, repeat, this minute and unmistakable description of the feeling that must be accepted as proof of pardon must be found in the word of God, as I suppose the time for a miracle in the case is past. No other testimony in the case will do, for no other witness than God is competent, no other witness is originally cognizant of the fact. But there is not a sentence to this effect in the word of God. In the absence of this unmistakable description of the feeling which should be accepted as proof of pardon, all that a happy experience proves is that the person is happy, happier, or happiest; this, and nothing more.

Another objection to any state of consciousness being taken as the evidence of remission of sins, is that we would not, in that case, have any obvious or *manifest* division line drawn between the world and the kingdom of God. Clearly, every one who *says* he has the required impression or feeling must be accepted. This does not seem to me so rational as it would be to have a rule or law of life and then infer that one is forgiven who complies with the law. Of course I know bad men can, in any case, impose upon us. Mark 2:3–12, says:

"And they come, bringing unto him a man sick of the palsy, borne of four. And when they could not come nigh unto him for the crowd, they uncovered the roof where he was: and when they had broken it up, they let down the bed whereon the sick of the palsy lay. And Jesus seeing their faith saith unto the sick of the palsy, Son, thy sins are forgiven. But there were certain of the scribes sitting there, and reasoning in their hearts, Why does this man thus speak? he blasphemeth: who can forgive sins but one, *even* God? And straightway, Jesus perceiving in his spirit that they so reasoned within themselves, saith unto them, Why reason ye these things in your hearts? Whether is easier, to say to the sick of the palsy, thy sins are forgiven; or to say, Arise, and take up thy bed, and walk? But that ye may know that the Son of man hath power on earth to forgive sins (he saith to the sick of the palsy), I say unto thee, Arise, take up thy bed, and go unto thy house. And he arose, and straightway took up the bed, and went forth before them all; insomuch that they were all amazed, and glorified God, saying, We never saw it on this fashion."

In this passage not only does Jesus establish the fact, in the only way in which it *can be done,* that he has power on earth to forgive sins, but incidentally he makes it plain that we may know that our sins are remitted by the.fact that he says so. In this case his *work* was offered as voucher for his word. As this mode of assurance, then, was good and satisfactory, so it is now.

After these definitions and qualifications of the terms of the general proposition I am ready to enquire:

2. *What is the meaning of the proposition: "Baptism is for remission of sins?"* I mean by it: 1. That God has a *law* for the forgiveness of sins; 2. That the sinner, who is responsible for compliance with the law, is not pardoned till he complies: 3. That baptism is in this law of God. I mean to assert that the predicate of

the proposition is, by the will of God, so related to the subject that it must be affirmed of it and not denied. I mean that remission of sins is conditioned, in the law of God, upon being baptized.

I mean that, one of the purposes or designs of being baptized is, remission of sins.

But as a definition is exclusive as well as inclusive; or, as it is necessary, in order to a clear view of a thing defined, to specifically separate or exclude from it whatever we do not wish to include that might otherwise be thought to be included,

I proceed to specify some things which I do not mean to include in the proposition.

What I do not mean by the proposition: "Baptism is for remission of sins."

(a) I do not mean that there is any natural fitness in the means to bring to pass the result; I do not mean that water takes away sins, or that there is inherent virtue in either the act of being baptized, or in the element into which a person is baptized, to remove sins. Our salvation is all of grace. There is no *merit* in us, nor in anything we can do, on the ground of which we deserve or may demand anything at the hand of God. Still, this fact is not inconsistent with the fact that God bestows his grace upon certain characters only, and upon these, only upon such terms as he may specify as pleasing to him.

{b) I do not mean that baptism, *by itself,* is of any value. A person who has not believed on the Lord Jesus Christ with all his heart, and who has not repented of his sins, need not, ought not to, cannot be baptized. Should such an one pass through the form, the thing is lacking and the form is less or worse than valueless. Without a previous conversion of mind and heart and a resolution so fixed and strong that it pervades the whole being, to live Godly in Christ Jesus, no mere act of being buried in water,

after a given formula of words, will do any good.

The charge used to be made that the teachings of the Christian Church, on the design of baptism, involve them in the dogma of water regeneration and in some cases its members have been charged with holding that baptism *alone* is sufficient to secure remission. But, such is not the truth and it never was. The fault in this case, or for making this misrepresentation has, no doubt, been, in some instances, our own. Many of our preachers, and perhaps most of them, at times, have been a little careless in their efforts to explain what was really true, but what, to the mind of *good men,* greatly opposed to the tenet being offered, was understood to be quite a different matter from what it was. The fault finder in this case is, and no doubt was at fault for not hearing better. It is probable, also, that the speaker was often, may be *as often,* to blame for not considering more carefully and fraternally the condition of his hearers. No speaker has cleared his skirts till he has done this. Let one speak to those who, in what is called religious experiences, is in the habit of seeing God, the Holy Ghost, Jesus Christ, angels, and even the devil, in the rational style of Jesus and his apostles, and it is at once as clear to them as a sunbeam that you have no religion, that you "deny the operation of the Spirit," etc. A half century ago this was true of a much larger number of religious people, relatively, than it is now, perhaps. But, the *disposition* is strong, even now, to see sights, and the number of those who are supposing that they see or otherwise experience miraculous manifestations of God in the conversion of their souls is by no means small, even in the most cultured sections of the country. Man naturally seeks *certainty* in matters religious, and when his intelligence is not sufficient to give him faith in the promises of God upon which he can satisfactorily trust, and by which, as a Christian, he can in every case walk, he will and must resort to visions and dreams. The wish to be certain we are right is, with truly Christian men, universal and unavoidable. It is precisely the teaching of God's word on that point.

The error in this case is not in wishing for certainty, nor in supposing that the gracious Father intends that we shall have it, but it is in not relying upon that which is the infallible proof of the fact, and betaking ourselves to silly dreams and such like superstitions, for the proof. So far, then, as we are fairly responsible for misrepresentations concerning us, our fault has been, and probably is, about this: Some of us have failed to state, with sufficient clearness and fullness, our positions, so that even badly informed or badly prejudiced persons could not avoid understanding us. Also, beyond doubt, we have had, as others, some unstable, reckless, really unconverted men in our pulpits, who, like Apollos, needed to be taught the way of the Lord more perfectly. But the charge of teaching or holding the dogma of baptismal regeneration cannot, in truth, be brought against us as a people, nor against any considerable number of us at all. In fact, there is much reason to think that, in all such cases, on all sides, there is more perversity of spirit than want of information at the bottom. There is but little if any reason why any moderately well informed person anywhere should be ignorant of any one of the leading teachings of the Church of Christ.

If they do not know they have ample means of knowing just what we do teach.

(F) I do not mean that no one *can be saved,* in heaven, who has not been baptized. I have never known anyone, looked upon as being a respectable teacher in the church, who so held. I except from the proposition infants, those who lived under a former dispensation, those who cannot, on account of sickness, be baptized, those who are on islands, in deserts, on crosses, at the

North Pole, and such like. These all I would exclude from the operation of the law of baptism for remission of sins, except in so far as they may be responsible for their inability to comply. Or, in general, I except all those who are unable to be baptized and are not responsible for that inability. For these, baptism is nothing; or rather, it is not for these, or any of them, at all, neither for remission of sins nor for any other purpose.

God does not legislate for those who, for any reason, are not able to obey his laws. He that would try to prove that baptism is not for the remission of the sins of one who *cannot be baptized* is a failure as a teacher. God never ordained baptism for such an one, for *any purpose.* He that infers from such cases that baptism is not for remission of sins to the one for whom it was ordained, is probably safe enough, whether baptized or not.

Chapter 3.
Objections Considered.

SOME very true and thinking persons, men of good education and much experience, have filed objections to, "baptism for remission of sins," founded upon certain scriptures, which to them seem to disprove it. A few samples of these let us, now, examine. John 3:16–18; also, verse 36. These scriptures, as read in the common version, seem, it is thought, to condition remission upon *faith only.* So, at least, they are understood by many. Now, since faith is *before* the *baptism* of any one *can occur,* according to the word of God, it follows that if one who has faith is then, at the first moment of having it, pardoned, baptism is not for remission of sins. I shall examine these passages in the light of objections, and in this light only, for the present. I begin with verse 15, and quote from the Nev/ Version: "that whosoever believeth may, in him, have eternal life." The idea is the same as if we should read: "whoever believes, in him may have eternal life."

The question in this case is: Does the believing put one "in him?" Or, is it that, the "life eternal," which the one who believes *may have,* is "in him?" If the former view be the true one there is some force in the passage, as an objection; if the latter be the true idea, there is none. If the former be the correct idea, the sentence should read: "whoever believes" into him, "may have eternal life;" if the latter, it should read: "whoever believes, in him may have eternal life;" that is, it is the one who believes, who, only, *may* have eternal life. Or, express it thus: The one who believes *may,* but no one else can, have life in him. I suppose Paul expresses the same idea when he says: "He that cometh to God must believe," etc. Or, there is no coming to God, no pleasing of God without believing.

Now, it seems to me that, if one is "in him" at the moment

he believes, it could not be said of him afterwards, "he *may* have eternal life." It ought not to be said to one who already has eternal life, that "he *may have*" it. It should be, *"he has"* not, *"he may have."* But in fact Jesus said, "he may have," not, "he has."

Again, if the intention had been to say that believing puts one "into him," the Greek should have been, *"eis auton"* not, as here, *"en auto."* I suppose Jesus teaches that "eternal life" is in him and that the one who believes may—has the privilege to—come and have it. This view is, I suppose, made certain at John i: 12. "But as many as received him, to them gave he the right to become children of God, *even* to them that believe on his name." It is seen that to receive him and to believe on his name are equivalent in meaning; so the one who believes to the extent or degree of being led into the kingdom of God, has the right to become a child of God. Not that he is a child of God while he is *only* a believer; but having the faith that leads to obedience he *may* have the blessing of *"eternal life."*

Read, to the same effect, John 20:30–31: "Many other signs, therefore, did Jesus in the presence of his disciples which are not written in this book; but these are written that you may believe that Jesus is the Christ the Son of God; and that, believing, you may have life in his name." It is distinctly taught herein that the believing is precedent to the *privilege* of having the life in his name. Or, that believing only prepares one for obtaining it.

Finally, read I. John 5:1: "Whosoever believes that Jesus is the Christ is begotton of God." This shows the spiritual status of the believer. He is *begotten,* only begotten. His birth has not yet taken place; he is not yet translated into the kingdom of God's dear Son, or he is not "in him." He is, when he believes "with the heart" ready for a birth which is required in order to be "in him."

The phrase, "in him," or, "in Christ," denotes, as it were, lo-

cation within. It denotes some such a connection as exists between a vine and its branch. One "in Christ" is so joined to him as
to draw spiritual life from him who, only, has it. Only the vine has
the life which the branch must have, else it can bear no fruit; it
must die. As a certain connection between a vine and its branch
is essential to the life and fruitfulness of the branch, so, a certain
connection between Christ and a man is necessary in order to
Christian life and fruitfulness. This connection with Christ is expressed by the phrase, "in Christ." Without attempting to make
this phrase answer, in every minute particular, to any certain
facts and states, it may, I think, be said with all safety, and briefly,
that the one who believes Jesus in every statement he has made,
who loves him in every fiber of his being, and who walks in all His
commandments, up to the full measure of what is possible to
him, is, I think *practically,* in him. But so far as any one is authorized to affirm of *another man* that he is "in Christ," his assertion
must be based on things as he sees them. If God demands faith
unfeigned, and repentance, and public profession of faith and
purpose, then, we are not authorized to receive and treat one as
in Christ who lacks any one of these things. And, so far as the one
who does the receiving is concerned, he must believe that he
sees in the one to be received these prerequisites, else he cannot
receive him, except it be in mere pretense, which is not receiving
him at all. Should he act otherwise, his conduct would be that of
one who assumes to be a law-giver, not a subject of the divine
government. It is sometimes asserted that one is "in Christ," or
may be, who has not been baptized. Whatever may, In fact, be
the end of a life that has been in accord with the will of God in
everything except in respect to being baptized, *we,* who are not
authorized to make, or to change the law, have no right to say or
to affirm of any one's case what God has not said of it. If God has
said that one is baptized into Christ, it is not a mark of fidelity to

the will of God in one to say that a person may be in Christ, baptized or not. If Jesus has said, "unless one is born of water and spirit he cannot enter into the kingdom of God," and he has, then, no one ought to say that one is or may be in the kingdom of God, who is not so born. But I dismiss this point for the present.

It should be carefully noted that the Bible does not say that one believing Jesus, or who believes any person or thing, has or shall have life or any other thing. Such view is wholly without scripture warrant, is against the word of God and is opposed to human philosophy. Believing alone is dead, according to both reason and revelation. But, does not Jesus say: "he who believes is not condemned?" No, no; there is no such language, in the word of God, as that. Again, did not Jesus say, "he that believeth the Son has everlasting life?" No, he did not. It is not of the one who believes simply or only that Jesus speaks, but of that one who believes, or, of those who believe *"in him"* 1 *'into him,"* or "upon him."

Of the one who only believes, whose faith is simply in the pure intellect, James says, his faith "is dead, being alone." Of him who only believes, but does really believe, who believes with the heart, Jesus says: "He may, in him, have eternal life." God gives us eternal life, but that life is in his Son. And so we must be "in him" (whatever that may mean), where this life is, before we can have it. Believing in the heart prepares one for entering *"into him."* One who has believed in his heart, and has believed into righteousness, has everlasting life. So, the one of whom Jesus says, "he has everlasting life," is the believer, it is true, but it is only he who has *"believed into righteousness "* or has believed to the doing of the will of God.

Believing, then, when and while it is alone, is dead.

When the believing goes to the heart, and when the thing believed captures the heart and resigns it to the will of God, this one is begotten of God. It is now his privilege to come "into him," to be born or water, as he has already been begotten of the spirit. Finally, when one's faith has been perfected by doing the will of God, he is "in him," "has eternal life," "is not condemned." It is of this last mentioned believer that Jesus says, he "has eternal life." The believing was *into the* Son.

The latter part of the same verse, John 3:36, confirms this view. It says: "But he that *obeys* not the Son shall not see life, but the wrath of God abideth on him. ' ' This, it seems to me, goes to show that the "believing into him," which is the condition of having everlasting life, mentioned in the forepart of the verse, includes obedience to him; or, the one who has the everlasting life, is the one who has believed and obeyed him.

Acts, 10–43, is often cited by persons eminent for their learning and piety, as proof that one's sins are pardoned on believing, simply. If they are, of course baptism is not a condition precedent thereto. The passage reads as follows: "To him all the Prophets bear witness that, through his name, every one that believes on him *(into him,* gr.) shall receive remission of sins." I do not admit that there is any difficulty, as touching our question at least, in this passage. There are no terms in it that in any way allude to the fact or that in any way assert, that our sins are forgiven simply upon faith. The sense of this scripture is: I. That remission of sins is through his name, or by means of Jesus Christ; so, that whoever refuses him as a savior must fail of salvation. And, 2. That this salvation, which is through the name of Jesus Christ, is his who believes "on him." (Into him, Gr.)

It is the case of the one mentioned by Jesus, John 3:36, who hath everlasting life; or, it is such as Paul alludes to, Heb. 10:39, where he says: "But we are not of them that shrink back unto perdition; but of them that have faith unto the saving of the soul."

Again, see John, 12:42: "Nevertheless even of the rulers many believed on him; but because of the Pharisees they did not confess *it,* lest they should be put out of the synagogue: for they loved the glory of men more than the glory of God." Here we have it stated that "many of the rulers believed 'on him; ' but because of the Pharisees they did not confess it, lest they should be put out of the synagogue; for they loved the glory of men more than the glory of God."

It is a fact that these rulers believed. It will not do to say that they did not really believe, that they only pretended or claimed to believe, for Jesus, who knew what the truth in the case was, says they believed. His testimony is direct; and in terms clear, unequivocal, he asserts that they believed. If faith had been the only requisite to secure for them a place among his disciples, or "in him," they were saved, were "in him," were his disciples. But, in fact, they were not his disciples, they were not in him. The context shows this. There is no proof that their faith was intellectually defective. Nor did their faith lack heart, altogether. The presence of "eis auton" (into him), following the expression, *believed,* and modifying it, proves that they had heart in believing; but the context shows that they did not have *enough* heart in it else they would have confessed him. It is, then, clear that intellectual believing, alone, does not secure the blessing; nor does heart faith either, unless there is *enough heart* in the believing to, morally, compel the believer to do the duty laid down in *the faith.* Whenever there is enough heart in the believer to morally compel the doing of duty, the faith saves, just as do the other parts of the requirements prescribed by the Lord Jesus, who, only, can save. All this makes it certain beyond the possibility of any reasonable doubt that believing was not, and that it is not the *only* condition of one's salvation or pardon.

Intellectual faith is necessary to forgiveness, but when and while it is alone it is worth nothing. Heart faith comes after this, and is, where it exists, an addition to it. But while these are alone they are of no value for this life or the next. The value of faith of whatever kind or degree, of head or heart, or both, is never found in itself; it is found in the "work of faith," or—which is the same thing—in the life ordered according to the faith. It is only as, and when, faith brings one into the will of God, or leads one to take Jesus' yoke upon him, that it is of value, otherwise it is of no worth to any soul of man.

It is held by some that the presence of *eis* (into) following "to baptize," does not prove that baptism takes a person into Christ, or that it is "for remission of sins." If this be true it would or ought to follow that the same preposition following, to believe and having for its object eternal life does not prove that faith is the alone condition precedent to having eternal life. That is, if, since we may believe into Christ, it follows that baptism may not be for remission of sins, it is for the same reason true, that, since we are baptized into Christ, it may follow that faith is not for remission of sins. These two statements are equally true. If to believe *eis auton* (into him) proves that faith is the alone condition of being "in him," then to be baptized "into him" *(ets auton')* proves that baptism is the alone condition of being "in Christ." While each of these hypotheses is equally true, they are both utterly false.

Matt. 26, 28: "For this is my blood of the covenant which is being shed for many unto *(eis)* forgiveness of sins." It is often held, and not in frequently urged in a spirit and style offensive to the taste of the highly cultured in spiritual matters that, it is the blood of the Lamb of God that cleanses from sin. If it be replied: Yes, of course I know that; what then? indignation often rises high, and the objector replies in much passion and ignorance: Why, it follows that baptism has and can have nothing to do In the matter of one's forgiveness. That is, the objector holds that when any one thing is said to be for remission of sins nothing else can be for that purpose; if the blood of Jesus is for remission of sins, then baptism cannot be. The absurdity of the view herein opposed is so glaring that one hesitates to make any reply. But, as it is hard to find anything so absurd that there are not multitudes ready to believe it; and as there are like multitudes ready to dispute the plainest truths addressed to the human understanding, so it would seem to be needful to give line upon line and precept upon precept, in regard to even the plainest matters.

Paul says: "We are saved by hope." Jesus shall "save his people from their sins." "Whosoever shall call upon the name of the Lord shall be saved." Speaking of his blood, Jesus says: "Which is shed ... for remission of sins." This list might be extended much. It is said, "Baptism now saves us, or you." Would it be a correct rule of interpretation to say: When it is ascertained from the scriptures that any one thing is for remission of sins, nothing else is to be allowed to be for remission of sins?

The Bible interpreted, throughout, by that rule is left so absurd and false that the Koran would be a gem in comparison with it.

But, this point is so entirely plain that it is not deemed necessary to enlarge upon it further.

Chapter 4.
Objections
Further Considered.

IT is sometimes objected against the proposition which I am affirming, that baptism is *outward,* and that no outward thing can be "for remission of sins." This objection is, by no means, well considered.

Is it thought, by the objector, that "remission of sins" is a great moral change in the feelings or sentiments of the heart, and that baptism, being outward, cannot be a condition of or a necessary antecedent to such a state of the heart, and that, therefore, it is not for "remission of sins"? Waiving controversy as to whether baptism might not have much to do with the conditions of the heart (the apostle Peter sets baptism in close correspondence with the conscience when he says that it "is the asking of a good conscience after God"), it is at least true and enough to say, that remission of sins and a great, radical heart change are by no means identical things. Such heart change is a necessary antecedent to and a condition of remission of sins. Indeed, one's faith must be, "as it were," baptized into a heart full of such changed sentiments ere it is a "faith into salvation." When one's faith is into life he is begotten. Now he has God's permission to become a child of God; or, to enter into Christ, to put on Christ, to be born into the kingdom of God.

Remission of sins is not to be inferred, as a fact, from any sensible event which may take place on or in a person; it is a rational affair that we grasp by faith, founded upon the word of God. It is God who remits sins. The time when and the conditions upon which he chooses to perform the deed are matters which

we may not, cannot, *a priori* know. These he determines for himself. There is no reason why God might not connect remission of
sins with the act of baptism quite as reasonably as with any other
act of the creature. It is true, as we have said, that baptism has
no virtue or efficacy, in itself considered, to remove sins. It is not
at all on this ground that we make our affirmation. Does the objector say that faith is, as a condition, for remission of sins? Faith
has no virtue or efficacy, in itself, to remove sins. It is the *work of
the creature,* as certainly and to the extent that baptism is. The
sinner *merits* nothing when he believes or because he believes;
nor does he when or because he is baptized.

Faith, when considered apart from every other thing, is a
purely *intellectual* act or state of a person. Christian faith, or faith
that is into life, is this purely intellectual act or state gone to the
heart, and is there warmed into life. There is yet *no merit* in it.

Is it held that, when one believes, and especially when he believes "with the heart" (or in the heart) he comes into harmony
with the will of God in respect to the very highest part of his nature? This is quite true. But is not this true of one also when he/
is scripturally baptized? Are not faith and heart both present
when one is baptized in accordance with the will of God? Nay,
more, are they not present in a more intense and working degree
than ever before? If they are not present when one is baptized,
then he is not, in truth, baptized at all, except in the sense that
one when drowned is baptized. Such a performance is not a
Christian baptism. Herein is seen the reason why an infant, having neither faith nor heart in the matter, is not and cannot be
baptized. A so-called baptism in such case is too entirely outward
to be of any value to the infant or of any service to God. But we
affirm our proposition, not on the ground that baptism is inclusive of both faith and heart, in that they are both intensely present in it, but on the authority of the word of God only. He, alone,

knows why and when he forgives sins, except as he has revealed these things to us. We know them only as we, by faith, rest in the word of God. The objection to our proposition, made on the ground that baptism is outward, is, therefore, not well taken.

Persons of respectable intelligence and of undoubted piety, have been known to object, on the ground that they *knew* their sins were pardoned before they were baptized. They could give the date of the happy event, even the very moment of its occurrence. They could not, therefore, regard baptism as an appointment or ordinance of God, "for remission of sins."

With them, the fact of pardon was not a matter of faith in God's word. Their assurance was conditioned, not upon knowing or understanding or believing the word of God or any part thereof; they avowed themselves as being *conscious* of the fact; therefore, they *knew* it to be true. A discussion with such an one of the question under consideration would be an absurdity. His one witness—consciousness—whose testimony is, with him, decisive of the question, whatever may be said by God, angels, or men to the contrary, is an *ex parte* witness. The witness asserts that his friend—himself—was, on a certain day, at a certain moment, pardoned; a thing which he, the witness, *could not know to be true,* since the act of pardon does not take place within the range of his (or its) possible knowing. To such a statement, the only possible, logical, reply is: The witness has knowingly lied, or he has stated falsely through being deceived. On no rational view of the case has such, so-called, testimony any bearing on the question in contest.

It is objected, that if baptism be for remission of sins, then, one's salvation is dependent upon the presence of third parties. And since the objector regards this as certainly an error, he therefore holds the hypothesis which he supposes involves it, to be an error also.

Let it be carefully noted that: 1. The Bible does nowhere say that one's salvation may take place without the presence of third parties. 2. It gives no account of any one's having been pardoned when and where there were not third parties present. 3. The Bible gives us no facts or principles from which such an inference is necessary or even probable. 4. It mentions the conversion of many thousands of persons, men and women, at times and places quite wide apart. These conversions, beyond a doubt, were all made in accordance with the will of God, and yet in every case where there is anything said on the point, it is made clear that third parties were present. 5. It is susceptible of satisfactory proof that *now* no person is ever converted without the presence or co-operation of third parties. 6. It is most distinctly taught by the spirit of God, *in the Bible,* that third parties are demanded, required, commissioned, qualified, and *sent* into all the world, to lost sinners, to be instrumental in their conversion from sin. Why were the prophets in the world if not that they should be instrumental in the salvation of men? God seems to have said in this fact that third parties were needed.

It is a maxim of law that a person intends to do what he does. This rule of common sense may be applied to the doings of God as well as to those of men. He did send third parties to sinners to convert them. In proof of this I cite the New Testament. Having converted the sinner in this way, both always and everywhere; and since God could not do, nor intend to do anything without a good reason, a perfect reason, it follows that there is a reason, never to be controverted without making a direct reflection upon God, for the presence of third parties at the conversion of sinners. Therefore, the objection to our position, on the ground that it requires the presence of third parties, in the conversion of sinners, is not valid.

The great magna-charta of salvation—the great commission—is a conclusive proof of our position.

Jesus, just ere he stepped from Olive's brow upon the chariot of ascension and was borne in glorious and joyous triumph up to the eternal mansions of the blessed, said to his chosen twelve:

Go into all the world and preach the gospel to every creature."

Why was this, if it was not because these third parties were, according to God's plan of salvation, necessary? The people must believe in order to be saved; they must hear in order to believe; the gospel must be preached that it may be heard; the people could not hear without the preacher, and he could not preach unless he should be sent. Such are the unmistakable teachings of "God's word" in regard to the salvation of the soul. So, it is God's plan to send third parties to sinful men, that they may hear the gospel, believe it, obey it, and be saved.. If one should desire that this point should be elaborated further, let him examine, with us, a few passages of the scriptures, further.

Matt. 16:19: "I will give unto thee the keys of the kingdom of heaven: and whatsoever thou shalt bind on earth shall be bound in heaven: and whatsoever thou shalt loose on earth shall be loosed in heaven." At this time Jesus was near the cross—the end of his earthly mission. As the Father had sent the Son into the world, so, now, he sends his apostles into the world. The Divine theory for salvation, was that henceforth whoever would hear the apostles, heard Jesus and the Father who sent him; and whoever refused to hear the apostles, refused, thereby, to hear Jesus and his Father. The gospel, with its ordinances, was committed to the apostles, and it was by them committed to faithful men, who should be able to teach others, also. See Mar. 16:16; II. Cor. 4:7; II. Tim. 2:2, etc.

These lessons lie patent on the very surface of the inspired word of God. After the apostles entered upon their work the duty of every one who would be saved was to enquire of them or of some faithful one, coming after them, who could tell him what is "appointed for him to do," or, "who should tell them words whereby they might be saved." It is easy to find fault with this position and say: "Those who are sent for might not be willing or able to go," or, "they might drop dead on the way," or, "the sinner might die before the teacher could be had," etc. Then comes the question: "Must the salvation of the soul be contingent upon the whim, the will, or upon some condition or circumstance of third parties?" t But well informed men, who are, in their hearts, loyal to God, do not talk that way. God knew all the facts, actual and possible, in regard to men for all time, when he gave us the Bible, and yet he made the presence of third parties necessary to the faith and obedience of the sinner in order to his salvation.

But what is the meaning of the quotation at the head of this paragraph? There may be questions raised in regard to some matters mentioned or alluded to in the passage that are not of easy explanation. As touching our position it seems to me to be entirely clear. Peter was to have the keys of the kingdom of heaven. This is .certainly true, whatever may be true as to the other apostles. The delivery to him of the keys must signify that the holder was, thereby, to have the power to bind and to loose as it respects the kingdom of heaven. Literally, it means that if one should come desiring to enter into the kingdom and Peter should loose the door for him, or, should open the way to him, then the way should, likewise, be opened to, him, into heaven. On the other hand, if the door should be closed and kept closed against him by the apostle Peter, it would be closed against him in heaven. So the people were given to understand that, if they would be saved, they must enter the kingdom here and expect to enter heaven hereafter, by way of the apostles—third parties. It is true, now and here, that no one can enter the kingdom of heaven except by or through the way pointed out by the apostles.

The way *may* be open to some who do not come by the apostolic road, where the fault arises from hard circumstances, which prevented them from finding the door, unlocked by the apostle Peter. It is probable that God knows how to manage such cases. It is certain that we do not. God, who is the law-maker—the Lord of the law—can, of right, go outside of the law if he sees fit. He has not authorized us to do so; and hence if we do so we sin. We are not only not authorized to preach that those who go not in through the way of apostolic ingress may nevertheless enter the kingdom, but we are actually cut off from the privilege of so preaching. For Jesus says: "Whatsoever you bind or loose on earth shall be bound or loosed in heaven." That statement is in force now, and it will be while the Christian Religion is in force on the earth.

Does one say: "But those apostles were only instruments in the hands of God for opening or closing the door of salvation?" Certainly, this is, no doubt, true; but still, the meaning cannot be less than that God's will was to be expressed through *them,* and that when it was so expressed, it would be binding and final on earth and in heaven. These third parties, or their teachings, which is the same thing, are now, as in apostolic days, necessary to the soul's salvation, if it is to take place according to the word of God. To this God has tied us, though He may not have tied Himself.

In connection with the foregoing citations and reasonings let the following passages be carefully considered: Acts 2:40; I. Cor. 4:15; I. Tim. 4:16; and James 5:20.

The apostle James asserts that one person *may* convert a sinner from the error of his way and save a soul from death. According to I. Cor. 4:15, the apostle Paul "begat the Corinthians through the gospel." According to Acts 2: '40, the apostle Peter exhorted his hearers to save themselves "from this crooked generation." According to I. Tim. 4:16, Timothy, by giving heed to certain things, might save "both himself and those who heard him."

Now, as the presence of third parties in the salvation of sinners is provided for in the word of God, so that no conversion is contemplated as taking place in the absence of such parties, it follows that the objection to our affirmation, made on the ground that it conditions the conversion, and therefore the salvation of the sinner, upon the presence of third parties, is not valid.

Chapter 5.
Definition and Mode of Proof

BEFORE entering, directly, upon the argument, I submit a few words on the subject of definition. If words, or thought bearers, are wrongly defined in a standard lexicon of a language, the learner, or speaker, or writer is apt to be carried into error, perhaps grievous, and even calamitous. One looks into a dictionary that does not carefully distinguish between the *meanings* of words and their metonymical or figurative uses, and he is about certain, if he be not a careful critic, to be confused and misled. He looks among the many, so-called, definitions of his word, selects one to suit his notion, which may not be *the* or *a* meaning of the word at all, and then proceeds to declare that Webster, Worcester, Richardson, or some standard lexicon sustains his view. So he is happy in the thought of being in good company and of carrying his point. But, the ground of his bliss is his ignorance of the fact that his definition, so suited to his case, and which gives him so great satisfaction, is no meaning of his word.

No document is of any value to a reader unless its words had, at the time of its composition, definite meanings, and unless they are used in these meanings.

The veracious author of a document will assume that his readers know the meanings of the words he uses, or that they have the means of knowing them, otherwise he would have no good reason for using them. True, one may *employ* a word in an unusual sense sometimes; but in all such cases the meaning must be obvious from the connection in which it is found, or, from some circumstance of its use, or the writer must have explained the sense in which he uses it *immediately* upon using it. Otherwise he has no right to use the word as he does.

One of the very brightest editors in our country, known to

me, says: "Many terms have two or more meanings that are carelessly interchanged in their use in discussion," etc.

Our lexicons define words, often, in a marvelously unscientific way, I think. Take the word ' "dip," for example, as in Webster: "Dip: 1. To plunge or immerse. 2. To immerse for baptism. 3. To wet, to moisten. 4. to engage or compromise; to mortgage." Now, who that thinks, believes that the word *dip* signifies: to wet, to moisten, to engage or compromise, to mortgage? True, one may be wet by dipping; but, he may be killed, or made sick, or cooled off, or scalded, or soaked, or cleansed, in the same way.

Must we conclude that, because by dipping a person these results may follow, therefore these are meanings of the word dip?

The Latin word, *Carpo,* signifies to pluck, pick, pull, etc. It is also defined: to pillage, to rob, to steal. A case is given in the books of a boy who entered a neighbor's orchard by a back way, and, without the knowledge and against the will of the owner, *carped* his apples. These are the facts in the case. In translating the Latin we say he *"stole* his apples." The boy plucked or pulled the apples. This is what the word *carpo* informs us that the boy did, and nothing more. It is not from the word *carpo* that we get the idea of stealing, for such an idea is not in it, and hence it ought not to be so defined. But this word and other words and circumstances, taken all together, make out a case.

When one attempts to give the meaning of a word he should give it as unaffected by any other word or circumstance whatever. The *character* of an act, or the results thereof, should not be taken as the definition of a word employed to *assist* in setting forth the facts of an act.

A tree is not often found to cast a shadow that is wholly unaffected by the shadow cast by any other tree. A reputation is scarcely ever found that is wholly that of any *one* given man or woman. So, not many words, in any composition, are found to have just their own and all of their own meaning, unaffected by any other word or circumstance in the connection. This word, *carpo,* names *one* prominent fact in this theft, viz.: to pull or to pluck, but no more, for it *has no more* to say. Of course the word is responsible for no more than what is contained in it. The boy plucked or pulled the fruit; and but for other facts in the connection stated he must be held to be entirely innocent of theft. Now, therefore, a lexicon that gives, *"to steal,'"* as a definition of *carpo,* is not in the line of legitimate lexicography.

A word, at a given time, has one and but one *current* sense. This one, current sense, *must* be the one accepted as its meaning at the time it was used in the book or document under consideration, in all places in said document where it is found, unless the connection does not permit it.

The meaning of a word in any given place is, *prima facie,* what its meaning is, when alone. A word has a sense when it is unaffected by any other word or circumstance whatever; that is, as it stands alone on a page otherwise blank. This meaning is *the meaning of the word.* Often, in composition, it seems to appear in a modified sense, sometimes in a very modified sense. In *such cases* the meaning which a given word seems to have is not a meaning of the word itself so much as it is the sense of the whole connection. In case the word, being considered, designates or stands for some prominent feature, circumstance, or part of the general transaction, the sense of the whole connection is, in translating or defining, often put on it.

In most cases, as for example where the boy is said to have stolen his neighbor's apples, truth does not suffer by such translating or defining.

What I claim is that the metonymical or figurative employment of a word, often in a sense but little, if at all of kin to the meaning of the word, ought not to be given or taken as a *definition* of the word, but only as an allowably free figurative *use* of the word.

In all cases where a word is employed, the presumption is that it has, in the place, its current meaning. If one denies this the burden of proof is on him.

If one must admit that words, generally, have two or more meanings each, and that the reader or hearer has a right to assume that any one of its so-called meanings is as legitimate or defensible as any other, in any given place of its occurrence, it would follow that no discourse or writing is of any certain value; that thoughts, in any effort that can be made to convey them to others, are quite as likely to be concealed as they are to be revealed, by the words that are used.

This, I believe, is a legitimate conclusion from the hypothesis. Then, that certainty which is so important in the matter of marriage, heirship, divorce, notes, bonds, mortgages, records of all kinds—deeds, letters, books, papers, and orders in regard to peace and war'—everything is at an end. Therefore it is assumed, in the following pages, that words have/ at a given time, one and but one current meaning, in any given instrument. This one, definite, current sense is the one to be accepted wherever the word is used unless the connection absolutely forbids it; and he who makes this assertion must prove it. Canon Farrar says: "It has been a terrible disaster to the Christian Church that she accepted without challenge these vicious principles of Talmudic interpretation. In the preposterous form of the *multiplex census* of scripture, the commentators, from the days of Origen down to modern times, practically adopted the old Jewish Pardes—the method of explaining scripture which divided it into the four regions of, Peshat, Remez, Daruch, and Sod, or the literal, inferential, homiletic, and mystic senses of the written word. In my *History of Interpretation*—the Bampton Lectures for 1885—I have shown the fatal influence which these false conceptions exercised for centuries over the science of biblical exposition. They have filled reams of forgotten commentaries with masses of teachings which, when not positively erroneous, are yet absolutely irrelevant to the original text. Much may be al lowed to the exigencies of moral and homiletic instruction, but it cannot be laid down too strongly that nothing should be offered as the interpretation of scripture except what can be legitimately shown to be the literal, historic, grammatical, and contextual meaning, together with such inferences as spring immediately and indisputably from that meaning. The books of scripture were written, as all books have always been written since the world began, with the object of being understood; and the starting-point of all real exposition must always be the sense which the words would have borne among those to whom they were primarily addressed."

Chapter 6.
Baptism is for
Remission of Sins.

Is this proposition true? that is, is the subject so related to the predicate that the latter must be affirmed of the former and not denied. The proof of this proposition, that reason demands and on which we are bound to accept of it and act upon it, must be: 1. Homogeneous with the proposition itself, and, 2. It must be sufficient in quantity.

1.   Whether our proposition be true or not, God knows; and, unless God shall in some way give us information on it, we do not and cannot know. That is, from the very nature of the case the proof of our thesis must come from God and not from men. Every question in respect to the faith, or to the worship of God, and any questions as to the grounds of our hope for the future, in this life or the life to come, must be referred, for settlement, to the word of God. This point cannot, well, be urged too often or too much. The interests involved, and the great liability of men's going astray and making void the word of God by their traditions, plead the necessity for the strictest adherence to this rule. The facts in the history of the two Catholic and of most of the Protestant churches are abundant, in proof of the necessity for observing this rule.

Whether the baptism of John was from heaven or was of men, was a question propounded by the Master to the "Chief Priests and the Elders of the people" of the Jews. They replied, "we cannot tell." Many in our day seem to think "it is of men."

Indeed, the controversy is now, as it has been in all the past, whether anything in the Bible should be held and regarded as being from heaven—or is it not all "of men." With those who hold the latter view, more or less distinctly, the healthy moral effect of a sturdy faith in the existence of a personal God, a Savior, the Holy Spirit, in the inspiration of the scriptures, in the reality of heaven, hell, and in a state of future rewards and punishments, is not possible.

2. On this division of the present chapter I need not enlarge much. The thoughtful reader will judge for himself whether, I. The evidence offered in support of the affirmation herein made is homogeneous with it or not; and, 2. Whether the amount of evidence offered is sufficient to establish the position taken.

3. Let it be agreed that our proofs must be from God, and that they must be pertinent and abundant. No mere man, unassisted, or uninspired, can possibly know the mind of God on this or on any like subject. I. Cor. 2:11–16.

But, when a portion of the scriptures is cited, in proof, what must such passage contain?

1. It must contain, in some way, the subject of our proposition—baptism. This term must be expressly mentioned; or, it must be so embraced in what is expressly mentioned that the inference that it is in the passage must be, not a merely possible one, but a necessary one.

When an inference, simply, may be drawn, it is always true that it may not be drawn. As long as it is true that an inference may, possibly, not be drawn, it is not proved that it should be drawn. And as long as it is not proved that it must be drawn, from given premises, logic requires nothing but a denial.

If he rely upon inference for his conclusion, the affirmant will, if he be a fair, truth-loving man, put his finger upon his proof passage and say: "though the term, baptism, is not specifically named in this, my proof text, still it is virtually mentioned, it is necessarily implied in the following words, viz.: (Then he will cite them.) In no other way may he expect to enlist the attention or merit the respect of an intelligent, truth-loving people.

Any attempt to speak in such general, indefinite terms, as, in the least to leave the point at issue obscure, or that would not make manifest the pertinence of what is offered in proof, is, *prima facie,* conclusive evidence of a want of candor. This, when it is manifest, is, or should be, the ruin of the guilty one.

2.   The phrase, "remission of sins," must also be present in the passage offered in proof. For, if the words "remission of sins," be not present, either in terms or by necessary inference, in the proof text, no such conclusion as we are affirming, can be drawn from it. *Nihil ex nihilo fit.*

3.   These two terms must be so related, in the proof passage, that the rules or laws of language require that the predicate must be affirmed, and not denied, of the subject.

Chapter 7.
Leprosy, Sin and the Will of God Regarding Them.

IT is probable that the Tabernacle and the services connected therewith, were, in some respects, typical of the Church of Christ, and of some things pertaining thereto. See Heb. 9:1–12.

"Now, even the first covenant had ordinances of divine service and its sanctuary, a sanctuary of this world.

"For there was a tabernacle prepared, the first, wherein were the candlestick, and the table, and the shew-bread; which is called the Holy .place. And after the second veil, the tabernacle, which is called the Holy of holies; having a golden censer, and the ark of the covenant overlaid round about with gold, wherein *was* a golden pot holding the manna and Aaron's rod that budded, and the tables of the covenant; and above it cherubim of glory overshadowing the mercy seat; of which things we cannot now speak particularly. Now, these things having been thus prepared, the priests go in continually into the first tabernacle, accomplishing the services; but into the second the high priest alone, once in the year, not without blood which he offereth for himself and for the errors of the people: the Holy-Ghost this signifying, that the way into the holy place has not yet been made manifest while as the first tabernacle is yet standing; which is a parable for the time *now* present; according to which are offered both gifts and sacrifices that cannot, as touching the conscience, make the worshipper perfect, being only (with meats and drinks and divers washings) carnal ordinances, imposed until a time of reformation.

"But Christ having come, a high priest of the good things to come, through the greater and more perfect tabernacle not made with hands, that is to say, not of this creation, nor yet through the blood of goats and calves, but through his own blood, entered in once for all into the holy place, having obtained eternal redemption."

Now, in view of this quotation, and of other scriptures, which I need not here recite, I believe it is reasonably certain that there is, at least, a striking analogy existing between the case of the leper and his treatment under the law of the leper, on the one hand, and the case of the sinner and his treatment under the law of God, in the new covenant, on the other.

I.   Leprosy was not and is not curable, in its more malignant stages, by merely human skill or power. So, none can forgive sins but God. I believe there is no case of a leper having been cured, mentioned in the Bible, except such as were cured by direct divine power; as the case of Naaman. II. Kings 5:1—14:

> "Now Naaman, captain of the host of the king of Syria, was a great man with his master, and honorable, because by him the Lord had given deliverance unto Syria: he was also a mighty man in valor, *but he was* a leper. And the Syrians had gone out by companies and had brought away captive out of the land of Israel a little maid; and she waited on Naaman's wife. And she said unto her mistress, Would God my lord *were* with the prophet that *is* in Samaria! for he would recover him of his leprosy. And *one* went in, and told his lord, saying, Thus and thus said the maid that *is* of the land of Israel. And the king of Syria said, Go to, go, and I will send a letter unto the king of Israel. And he departed, and took with him ten talents of silver, and six thousand *pieces* of gold, and ten changes of raiment. And he brought the letter to the king of Israel, saying, Now, when this letter is come unto thee, behold, I have *therewith* sent Naaman my servant to thee, that thou mayest recover him of his leprosy. And it came to pass, when the king of Israel had

read the letter, that he rent his clothes, and said, *Am* I God, to kill and to make alive, that this man doth send unto me to recover a man of his leprosy? Wherefore consider, I pray you, and see how he seeketh a quarrel against me. And it was *soy* when Elisha the man of God had heard that the king of Israel had rent his clothes, that he sent to the king, saying, Wherefore hast thou rent thy clothes? let him come now to me, and he shall know that there is a prophet in Israel. So Naaman came with his horses and with his chariot, and stood at the door of the house of Elisha. And Elisha sent a messenger unto him, saying, Go and wash in Jordan seven times, and thy flesh shall come again to thee and thou shalt be clean. But Naaman was wroth, and went away, and said, Behold, I thought, He will surely come out to me, and stand, and call on the name of the Lord, his God, and strike his hand over the place, and recover the leper. *Are* not Abana and Pharpar, rivers of Damascus, better than all the waters of Israel? may I not wash in them, and be clean? So he turned and went away in a rage. And his servants came near, and spake unto him, and said, My father, *if* the prophet had bid thee *do some* great thing, wouldest thou not have done *it?* how much rather then, when he saith to thee, Wash, and be clean? Then went he down, and dipped himself seven times in Jordan, according to the saying of the man of God: and his flesh came again like unto the flesh of a little child, and he was clean."

Mark 1:40–44:

"And there cometh to him a leper, beseeching him, and kneeling down to him, and saying unto him, If thou wilt, thou canst make me clean. And being moved with compassion, he stretched forth his hand, and touched him, and saith unto him, I will; be thou made clean. And straightway the leprosy departed from him, and he was made clean. And he strictly charged him, and straightway sent him out, and saith unto him, See thou say nothing to any man: but go thy way, shew thyself to the priest, and offer for thy cleansing the things which Moses commanded, for a testimony unto them."

2.   The leper was not allowed to be among God's people, but when the fact of his leprous condition was known to exist, he was removed from among them. So it *should be,* now, as to the sinner. Then, there were persons whom God had appointed whose duty it was to watch for cases of leprosy; and when found, the lepers were removed. So it should be now, as to the sinner in the church.

3.   There were, no doubt, many cases of incipient leprosy that recovered. The priests were to watch such cases and to keep the parties confined. Not until the priest decided that the leprosy was gone, or, that the leper was clean as respects the leprosy itself, did the "law of the leper" require any duty or thing to be done by any one, except, in cases where the leprosy persisted, the priest must then have the leper removed.

But when it was decided that the leprosy was gone, the leper was still unclean and must suffer continued separation from the fellowship of God's people and all blessings pertaining to such fellowship until, according to the law of the leper, he became clean. See Lev., chapters 13, 14.

When the leprosy was gone and the leper was declared to be clean, he was to procure two birds, etc. (see Lev. 14:1–32), for his cleansing. Among the things that the leper had to do, in order to his being clean, was the bathing of his whole flesh in water. The antitype to this bath of the leper, if it have any, is the baptism of the sinner—the bath, or laver, of regeneration. There was no ceremonial cleansing of one under Moses, without a bath of the whole flesh in water, whatever the cause of the uncleanness might be. The law provided for, or required many sprinklings *of* blood, and of blood mixed with water, but there were no sprinklings of water unmixed. These sprinklings did not point to our baptism, but rather to the sprinkling of the blood of Jesus, the blood of the new covenant. See Heb. 12:24, *et al.* No one, under the law, having been unclean, was allowed the privileges and blessings of God's congregation until, besides other duties performed, he had bathed his whole flesh in water. Though they were without actual leprosy, yet they were unclean. This fact worked no hardship; but, even if it had, it would not have been a safe or wise thine to have objected to it and set it aside on that account. Had the leper come before Moses and said: "Moses, Aaron says I have no leprosy, it is gone. Now, there is no reason why I should be delayed from being among the brethren, and especially from seeing my family. This bath, etc., is a mere form, outward form. It does not stop the progress of, nor actually remove the leprosy. I suppose I might just as well walk into camp. Besides this, Moses, you ought to see that persons might be lepers where they could not get a priest, nor hyssop, nor birds, and where no water could be found. Moses, you surely do not hold that one is to be kept away from the society of God's people, from the tabernacle service, where is the priest, the high priest, the brazen altar, the laver, the seven-bowled golden lamps of God, the shew-bread, the censer, the ark of the covenant, the mercy seat, the angels, and the shekina! The having of these blessings, Moses, cannot possibly be suspended upon one's being bathed in water! Besides, the water might not be accessible, or it might be very cold; it might cause one's death to do this thing. Moses, do you not really mean that persons had better, in your judgment, do this thing who are in good health and feel like doing it? It is not essential, at all? Besides all these things, Moses, do you not see that millions and millions of persons would or might be forever deprived of these precious blessings of God if their having them should be made to depend upon the observance of a mere outward ordinance? It cannot be. Out upon such a religion."

What may we suppose that Moses would say to such an one? He would, I presume, reply about as follows: "God has made the order to which you refer. It is not mine to make or to unmake law in such cases. 'Who art thou that repliest against God?'"

The fact that, in cases of leprosy, the leper was to be, decided to be "healed of his leprosy" *before* he had any duty to perform, is regarded by some as being typical evidence that, now, one's sins are to be forgiven before he ought to be baptized. But this conclusion is founded on a misconception of the point of analogy in the parable. The likeness does not hold between the *removing of the leprosy* of the leper on the one hand, and the removing of the sinner's sins, on the other, but it is between the *cleansing* of the leper, *after his actual leprosy is gone,* and the *forgiveness of the sinner's sins.*

The sinner now is the leper under Moses; the sins of the sinner now, are the leprosy then. The forgiveness of the sinner now, is—not the cleansing of the leper from his leprosy, but—the cleansing of the leper whose leprosy is already gone. Then, says one, leprosy, in this type, corresponds to the sin of the sinner, and as the leprosy of the leper was certainly gone before the bath that was for his cleansing, so it seems to follow from this typical reasoning that the sinner's sins are or must be gone before he is baptized. Therefore, baptism is not for remission of sins, it is thought.

Let us see. Sin may be, and it is, in fact, in the Bible, considered under two aspects. 1. It is to miss the mark or way, and, in respect to serving God, it is to do what he forbids or to refuse to do what he requires. 2. It signifies certain *results* to the sinner, of violating the law of God. Sin, in the former sense, is never, in the

Bible, said to be forgiven. It is not forgivable, in this sense. Therefore, even God does not forgive sins, in this sense of the word. In the nature of the case He cannot. Of course, says some thoughtful man, God does not, literally, forgive, that is, send away, an *act* of transgression or disobedience of his law, but he may and does, in the case of pardoning the sinner, forgive certain *effects* or *consequences of* his sin. In this sense is God said to forgive sins, and in this sense only.

The effects of sin on the sinner are: 1. He is guilty. 2. He is liable to the penalty of sin. So, as it was under the law of the leper that the bath, besides other duties performed, was not to remove the leprosy of the leper, but, as a divinely appointed condition, it was for the removal of certain effects of the leprosy, and for restoring him—the leper—to the family of God, with all the blessings thereof; in like manner baptism is not for the removal of actual sin, but, as a divinely appointed condition, it is for the remission of certain effects or consequences of sin.

2. Jesus healed a leper. Mark I: 40–45: "And there cometh to him a leper, beseeching him, and kneeling down to him, and saying unto him, If thou wilt, thou canst make me clean. And being moved with compassion, he stretched forth his hand, and touched him, and saith unto him, I will; be thou made clean. And straightway the leprosy departed from him, and he was made clean. And he strictly charged him, and straightway sent him out, and saith unto him, See thou say nothing to any man: but go thy way, shew thyself to the priest, and offer for thy cleansing the things which Moses commanded, for a testimony unto them. But he went out and began to publish it much, and to spread abroad the matter, insomuch that Jesus could no more openly enter into a city, but was without in desert places: and they came to him from every quarter."

Jesus cleansed him, and told him to go and show himself to

the priest, "and offer for thy cleansing those things which Moses commanded, for a testimony unto them." Here, at the touch of Jesus, the leprosy "departed from him and he was cleansed." That is, he was cleansed from actual leprosy. Still he was not cleansed from the effects of it; he was still unclean. He could not return to the camp of Israel and enjoy fellowship with God's chosen people till he should comply with the law of the leper, as prescribed through Moses. These offerings which he was to make were not to cleanse him from the leprosy but from certain effects of it.

Chapter 8.
Israel Delivered from Bondage

IT is, I believe, generally allowed that the deliverance of Israel from Egyptian bondage was typical of the deliverance of the sinner from the bondage to sin. See Ex., chapters 14, 15, and I. Cor. 10:1–4. There is certainly a striking likeness between the two. Moses was a child with whom God's hand was from birth. So was Jesus. Jesus was the prophet the Lord our God raised up like unto Moses. Moses was mediator of the old covenant; Jesus was the mediator of the new. Moses entered the territory of those whom he would deliver, sent, directly, of God. So did Jesus. Moses went, armed with miraculous power, which he displayed before the people as proof that he was sent of God to deliver them from bondage. So Jesus came to the sinner and manifested by signs, wonders, and miracles that he was from God, sent to deliver him from the bondage of sin. The people would not follow Moses till they believed. They could not, and they ought not. So it is in regard to following Jesus Christ. They believed Moses and resolved to follow him, and did follow him to the Red Sea. So, now, one believes Jesus, or has faith, and *resolves to follow him*—repents—and to this extent, does follow him. But Israel was not yet delivered, completely, from bondage when they had believed Moses and had resolved to follow him, and had come to the Red Sea. So the sinner's salvation is not yet complete when he has believed, and resolved to fallow Jesus (repented). Moses, standing on the shores of the sea with Pharoah and his hosts pressing hard upon Israel, said, Stand still and see the salvation of God. Moses was commanded to stretch forth his hand over the waters, which he did, and they were divided and Israel was "baptized into Moses in the cloud and in the sea." On the other side—after their baptism—they were to see their former masters, no more. Their masters were destroyed and they were free. So sin, to which the sinner is in bondage, is not gone till the sinner is baptized. This is the force of the type, if there be a type in the case. Then their passage of the Red Sea was their baptism *into Moses.* I. Cor. 10:2. Now, our baptism puts us into Jesus Christ. Gal. 3:27.

Then, Israel did not understand that their salvation was complete, nor did they rejoice in the salvation of God till they were "all baptized into Moses in the cloud and in the sea." See Ex. 14:28, to 15:1, 2. So now, no sinner, under the reign of Jesus Christ, or after Pentecost, is mentioned anywhere in the New Testament as rejoicing in the faith that his sins were forgiven him, *till after he was baptized.*

Chapter 9.
The Baptism of John.

THE, SO called, John's baptism, was not, exactly, Christ's baptism. Still, it was from heaven and was not of men. God sent John to preach and to baptize. Thus he was to prepare a people for the Lord; thus he was to manifest the Christ to Israel, as the Son of God. In "preparing a people for the Lord" he baptized them. This baptizing had one purpose, or more than one, certainly. Those who rejected the baptism of John rejected the counsel of God against themselves. Those who would be baptized, but who were not, in faith and heart, ready for it, were rejected.

As a very suggestive and forcible lesson pointing to the conclusion that John's baptism was for remission of sins, I cite Matt. 3:13–17:

> "Then cometh Jesus from Galilee to the Jordan unto John, to be baptized of him. But John would have hindered him, saying, I have need to be baptized of thee, and comest thou to me? But Jesus answering said unto him, Suffer *it* now: for thus it becometh us to fulfil all righteousness. Then he suffereth him. And Jesus, when he was baptized, went up straightway from the water: and lo, the heavens were opened unto him, and he saw the Spirit of God descending as a dove, and coming upon him, and lo, a voice out of the heavens, saying, This is my beloved Son, in whom I am well pleased "

The facts in this case are that Jesus came "from Galilee to the Jordan to John to be baptized by him." But John made objection, on the ground that he had need, rather, to be baptized by Jesus. In reply, Jesus said: "Suffer it now, for thus it becometh us to fulfill all righteousness." Then he suffered him.

One who considers all these facts carefully, would not, prob-ably, be inclined to think that this righteous thing is a small thing, or an unimportant matter. Jesus walked twenty-five or thirty miles to attend to it, and then insisted on its being done, remind-ing John that it was a duty devolved upon both of them; for, so must the phrase: "thus it becomes *us* to fulfill all righteousness," be understood. John objected. Why did he object? He had just refused to baptize many of the Scribes and Pharisees who came to his baptism. In that case the objection was made on the ground that those who sought to be baptized were not penitent. John demanded that they should show signs, or give evidence of repentance before he could baptize them. "Bring forth fruit wor-thy of repentance," said the faithful wilderness preacher.

You, said he, put your claim, of right to be baptized by me, on the ground that you are Abraham's seed; but I require, in order that you may be baptized, that you shall repent of your sins and confess them. So, it seems that John was baptizing persons who, though sinners, had repented and confessed. Following this is the account of Jesus' baptism.

When Jesus came to John he did not come as one who had been a sinner, who had repented, confessed, etc. Therefore John did not see the reason why he should baptize him. John held that he had need to be baptized by Jesus, "and comest thou to me?" This question, put by John, must, I think, mean that he did not understand himself to be baptizing persons who were pure or sinless, as was Jesus. I suppose any other one who should have appeared to be entirely free from sin, would have been rejected, as Jesus was. So the way is quite open to the conclusion that the baptisms of John were for remission of sins, with a decided lean-ing of the facts in that direction. John was in the habit of baptizing such persons, and such only, as confessed their sins. Of course Jesus could not do this, hence John's refusal.

As something supposed to be out of harmony with the view here taken, if not suggestively against it, as some suppose, I will cite and examine Matt. 3:11: "I, indeed, baptize you, in water, unto *(eis)* repentance."

This passage is not without its difficulties. It is held, by some persons, that John's baptism was for the purpose of bringing the people into repentance; that repentance was *a,* and perhaps *the* end to be reached by the baptism. This conclusion is supposed to be justified, if not forced upon us, by the fact, here stated, that John baptized his disciples *(eis metanoian)* "into repentance." It is, therefore, thought that his baptism was before repentance and in order to it. It is held that their act of being baptized was a committing of themselves to do, after their baptism, what, by the hypothesis, they had not done before; that is, to repent. This view is, I suppose, wholly indefensible, so much so that God cannot, by any means, be regarded as the author of it. No man, who is strictly honest, can give a pledge or obligation, in any form, that he will, at a future time, repent of his sins. He may *say* that he will repent tomorrow, but he does not tell the truth; he does not mean to do it. We may do things, and things may be done for us, to insure or to induce larger measures of sorrow for sins and fix our purposes more firmly to live the *life* of those who are now penitent for all past sins, and who are now resolved, in case of sinning in the future, to turn away from it, and live lives of penitent devotion to God, more and more as the days are going by, yet, in all such cases, repentance does precede, though it should be expected, designed, and required to follow the thing or things done.

The word repentance is defined by Webster as follows: "The act of repenting, or the state of being penitent." This distinction between the *act* of repenting and the *state* of being penitent is certainly a correct one. The absurdity of supposing that one might be baptized into repentance in the former sense is so readily seen that a mere statement of the case carries the correct conclusion with it.

It would seem, then, that the baptism of John must have put persons into a "state of being penitent." But before one can be in a "state of being penitent" he must have, already, repented. In any defensible view whatever, the act of repentance was before the baptism in the case of each one who was baptized. It seems to me, therefore, that the baptism that is said to have been "into repentance" was, to the baptized party, into *estate* of repentance. But, as the one baptized was, already, so far *as his own* heart and spirit were concerned, in a state of penitence, it follows that his baptism did not induce these conditions in him, or put *him* into them. Then, it seems that, as the baptism was, certainly, "into repentance," and as the party being baptized had already repented, and as to himself, was already in a state of penitence, the baptism is herein declared to have had the effect of bringing the baptized persons into formal and visible connection with the cause which John preached and with the people whom John was making ready for the Lord. The preacher's cry in the wilderness was: "Repent, for the king of heaven is at hand!" Turn you, turn you, or, repent, turn, was the text of John the Baptist. It was his text, not for one sermon only, but always and every-where. Now, when persons went to John and showed satisfactory signs of having repented and were then baptized, they occupied the position of the penitent and waiting ones. It was, I presume, into this state of penitence and waiting that John baptized the people. The distinguishing feature of John's preaching was that the people must repent else they could not be accepted by John, nor of God. Jesus and his disciples preached the same thing and in the same way, till the crucifixion. That ordinance, by means of which the baptized were designated as having accepted the call to repentance, as preached by John, might very well be said to be "into repentance." There are some other views taken of this passage by very true men of high attainments, but it is not deemed necessary to discuss them here. Whatever needs to be said more can be conveniently introduced into the examination of the following passages:

Mark 1:4: "John was baptizing in the wilderness, preaching a baptism of repentance *(eis)* into remission of sins." Luke says, 3:3: "And he went into all the regions round about the Jordan preaching a baptism of repentance *(eis)* into remission of sins." It is seen that both of these writers say the same thing; viz., that John announced "a baptism of repentance into remission of sins." John was the herald sent before the coming Lord to prepare his way and to make ready a people for him at his coming. He announced the kingdom of heaven at hand, and he exhorted all who would be HIS friends, who would enter into the kingdom and receive HIS blessings, to speedily make the requisite preparations.

Hitherto citizenship in the commonwealth of Israel had been conditioned upon descent from Abraham and circumcision, or, in the case of foreigners, upon being bought with the money of a Jew, etc. Now, these conditions were being set aside, a new government is being introduced, a spiritual reign over the true Israel, the spiritual sons of Abraham. John was commissioned to declare to the people what they must be and do in order to enjoy the privilege of citizenship in this new kingdom "at hand." In discharging this duty Mark says he preached "a baptism of repentance *(eis) into remission of sins."*

Observe this passage does not say that he preached repentance for remission of sins. Though, without repentance there is, of course, no remission of sins, yet this scripture does not announce the necessity of repentance in order to remission, except, possibly, by implication. The declaration is that he preached a baptism into, and therefore in order to remission of sins. Yet, it was not a baptism alone or by itself that he preached, but it was a baptism "of repentance," qualified by repentance. The Greek is, *"baptisma metanoias"* translated, a baptism of repentance. *Metanoias* is a noun in the genitive case, which case indicates origin or source, whence the notion or principal thought in the sentence is derived.

W. E. Gelf, in his "Grammar of the Greek New Testament," Vol. IL, page 153, third edition, says: "The genitive expresses the antecedent notion, that notion which precedes the principal verbal notion, in the series which forms the whole thought." And on page 199, same vol., he says: "when two substantives are so joined together that the one seems to depend upon and derive its force and meaning from the other, in any one of the relations given above, that substantive on which the one depends, is in the genitive, as being in some respect antecedent to the proper conception of its state or nature, and hence arises the rule that when two substantives are joined together, the one that explains and more accurately defines the other, is in the genitive, as it is the expression of some notion whence the notion of the other substantive springs."

Buttman, in his Greek grammar, section 132, page 330, says: "In order to comprehend the genitive in its full syntactical relations, especially with verbs, we must premise that the fundamental idea of the genitive is that of SEPARATION, a *going forth,* whether out of the interior of anything, or from its exterior; and that, therefore, the idea of the prepositions *ek,* out of the interior, *apo,* from the exterior or side of an object, is primarily in the genitive case itself."

Winer's "Grammar of the Greek New Testament," page 184, says: "The genitive is acknowledged to be the whence case (the case denoting source, departure, or descent; cf. Hartung, Casus,

§ 12), and is most clearly recognized as such in connection with words expressive of action, and accordingly with verbs. Its most common and most familiar appearance in prose, however, is in connecting two substantives; here, through its gradually extended signification, it denotes every sort of *dependence* or *belonging.*"

Harrison, "Greek Prepositions," page 15, says: "The simplest case, apparently, at least, of the use of the genitive in Greek, is that in which, corresponding to the English "of," it is employed to qualify the preceding noun, and to show in what more definite sense it is to be taken. "Louisville Debate," page 253.

Moses Stuart, "Grammar of the Greek New Testament," page 161, says: "The fundamental idea in this case has already been shown (in •§ 96); it is the *whence case.* This general idea may be applied to *space, time,* and finally to *causality* or *originating source,* in its most extensive sense."

Thus we see that the primary and essential notion expressed by the genitive case is antecedent in its character and not consequent; that it looks *back* to some source or beginning out of which the principal or leading notion, *in* the *sentence,* takes its rise and from which it derives its value or by which it is modified. In the light of these authoritative statements of the law of the genitive case in New Testament Greek, I conclude that the repentance of the passage is clearly not that which is here declared to be into remission of sins. That is, it is not the object of the writer to declare that repentance is into remission of sins, but rather to say that out of it the baptism, in a sense, must spring; or, that the desire to be baptized must have its origin in the fact that one had repented, else it would not be the baptism that John was announcing for, or into, remission of sins.

It is sometimes said that preaching is for remission of sins, that heading is also; that being born is in order to remission of sins, since no one can have remission of sins without first having been born, etc. Yes, I suppose it is also necessary that one should commit sin before he could obtain the remission of his sins. Such talk is the veriest trifling. The question for us here is, What does the inspired writer mean by what he says in this verse? It is certain that he declares something to be for remission of sins. Is it the repentance in this passage that is said to be for remission of sins?

We have shown that the repentance *of this passage* looks not forward to an object, but looks back as a qualifier to some antecedent notion, which is, in this case—baptism. This antecedent notion, the writer says, has its origin in repentance, and is for, or into, remission of sins. Baptism is for remission of sins, but not of itself, or by itself; for it must look to repentance and see that, out of it, it had its origin. This is not only the grammatical force of the genitive, *metanoias,* but it is historically true that repentance bears the relation to baptism which is here indicated. At the fifth verse of this chapter it is said that the people "were all baptized by him in the river Jordan, 'confessing their sins.'" The confessing was, I suppose, before the baptism, and it is certain that repentance precedes all confession of sins. According to this view, the baptism of the people was preceded by and conditioned upon their repentance. Indeed, their de sire to be baptized grew out of the fact of their repentance—their sorrow for sins, their resolution to abandon them, and their willingness to use the means appointed for remission. If it be said, the confessions in these cases were implicit, not explicit; or, that they were implied in the fact of their baptism, but that they were not formally made in order thereto, my answer is: This is very doubtful, if not improbable.

But, for our present purpose, it matters not which view is the correct one. Each, alike, requires that repentance should have *preceded* the baptism. John preached repentance (Matt. 3:2) as well as baptism, and when certain of the Pharisees and Saducees came to his baptism, he seems to me to have demanded some evidence of the fact that they had repented, in order that the baptism might be so qualified as to be "the baptism of repentance into remission of sins." So I conclude that whether the confession of sins and declaration of repentance took formal shape before baptism or not, it is at least true that the repentance preceded the baptism and was a necessary qualification of it.

Having seen that the Harbinger preached a baptism *of repentance,* a baptism qualified by repentance, the question arises: What was the design of it? Of course, it had some design. The great majority of those who profess to serve God do now say, and they have in all the past eighteen centuries said, that the baptism of John was for *(into)* remission of sins; they have held that the Greek phrase, *"eis aphesin hamartion "* should be rendered for, in order to, or, into remission of sins. A few persons have, during a comparatively late period, contended that the baptism of this passage was to have been submitted to on account of a fact already accomplished, or of an end already reached, and not in order to an end *to be reached.* This latter view not only contradicts the rules of language, which are founded on the nature of the human mind, but it contradicts the teachings of the word of God, as I understand things.

Does this phrase, *"eis aphesin hamartion,"* give the reason or ground on account of which the baptism might or should take place? If so, the translation ought to be, "because of remission of sins." Does this phrase state the object, purpose, or end to be reached by the one who seeks the baptism of repentance? Then it should be translated: for, or, in order to, or, into, remission of sins. I suppose it does, certainly, the one or the other. Let us look at the former hypothesis. If the phrase in question gives the reason or ground of the baptism; that is, if what is stated in the phrase is supposed to have been already attained, and on this account the person who has "remission of sins," is entitled to be and ought to be baptized, it would follow that the fact of remission of sins is to be taken as the reason why the one having it should repent, which is here declared to be a qualification for the baptism. That is, the people were called upon to both repent and be baptized, because their sins were forgiven. I do not see that receiving the remission of sins is any reasonable ground for repentance. So long as it is and always was and must be true that repentance is necessarily antecedent, and in order, to, remission of sins, it cannot be that remission is prior to and is the reason or ground of repentance. Hence the interpretation of this passage that makes remission of sins already enjoyed the ground of repentance and baptism, is not the true one.

Moreover, the preposition, *eis,* which shows the relation between the act of a penitent's being baptized and the remission of his sins, has no such meaning as would justify us in supposing that the sinner must first enjoy the remission of his sins, and then and therefore, repent and be baptized.

Ex-President W. K. Pendleton, in "Christian Quarterly" for April, 1870, pages 148, 149, says:

> "While *eis* may be translated by so many different words and phrases, it never loses its proper meaning of 'in,' 'within.' This is its force everywhere, namely: *That the subject (that is, the true, logical subject} between which and something else this preposition is used to express a relation, comes or is brought to be 'in, ' 'within, ' that something else.* Dr. Harrison says: 'When *eis* is added to the action or motion of the verb, or to any substantive idea that may imply these, and regard is had to the accusative case following, there arises from the conjunction of the preposition, with its sense of 'in,' and 'within,' of the action or motion of the verb with its now

defined direction, and of the accusative case, with its
power of marking the limits within which the action or
motion is confined the sense of 'into,' and the effect is to
represent the subject of the action or motion as brought
within the *circumscribed space, class, or category y state,
or circumstances named by the noun in the accusative?*
(Page 221.) This statement describes precisely the circumstances which are found in the passages which we
have under discussion. Let us apply it to them. We begin
with Mark's statement about John, that 'he came
preaching the baptism of repentance *eis* the remission of
sins.' Here the phrase, 'baptism of repentance,' is described by *eis* as having a relative direction of 'in, '
'within,' *a terminus ad quern;* the accusative case—'remission of sins '—denotes the object with regard to
which it has this relative direction, and the effect is to
represent the person who is the subject of the baptism
as brought 'into ' or within the state or circumstances described by 'remission of sins.'

"The passage in Acts 2:38, requires the same explanation. The command of Peter, 'Repent and be baptized,' is
made by *eis* to point in a *certaindirection;* not 'around,'
'above,' or 'beneath,' but 'in,' 'within; ' and the circumscribed limits of this direction are defined by the accusative to be *the remission* of sins. The baptism looks to this,
and nothing else, and the effect is to represent the subject of baptism as brought into or within the condition
described by the logical *accusative*—'the remission of
sins.'"

Mr. Jelt, in his "Greek Grammar," Vol. II., page 296, says of
eis:

"It expresses the same relations as *en,* except that it
has the notion of a direction—*whither*—while *en* has the
notion of rest—*where.* It is used to express the direction
or motion of an action—into an object, or up to an ob-

ject—into immediate contact with it; especially to express the reaching of some definite point."

Such, according to this authority, which is among the very best, is the meaning of the word which sets forth the relation between the baptism of John, which was a "baptism of repentance," and remission of sins. In the light of the above definition of *eis,* it will not do to say that the baptism of this passage, qualified as it is, and as it had to be in order to be the baptism that John preached, is to take place in view of something that had already transpired, affording the reason or ground for it. The force of *eis, which never looks back to a ground or reason,* but always looks forward to some pur pose or end to be reached, forbids this view. And since this view is not admissible it follows that the only other theory taken by any one, so far as I know, is the true one—the baptism of John was "for, or into, remission of sins." Q. E. D.

Deeming a thorough examination of this passage to be of much importance in our argument, I paused at this point and addressed the following note to Chas. Louis Loos, President of Kentucky University, who is very eminently qualified to speak on the subject:

> "Is *meianoias,* in Mark 1:4, a case of the objective genitive? If so, why; if not, why not? Also, give me your idea of the meaning and force of *eis* in the same passage."

To this note, which is given here only in substance, I received the following reply:

> Mark 1:4. baptisma metanoias eis aphesin hamartion. "There is nothing in the form of the expression *bap. metanoias,* to indicate whether it is the objective or subjective genitive. These varieties of the genitive are not always, or even generally, determined by the form; the connection, with other accompanying words, decides this matter. It is hermeneutically, as well as philologically,

that such distinctions are discovered; it is a logical question, chiefly. Furthermore—the terms objective and subjective, do not always—very often not—describe well the true nature and office of the genitive—too remotely and obscurely often to be clear to the inquirer. If we look into the Greek grammars we will find other more specific and intelligible, and much more truly descriptive definitions. So in this case. The proper designation of the genitive here is the *characteristic, qualifying*—describing the *character* of the *baptisma*—a very general use of this case.

"Now, when we say *'characteristic, qualifying,'* we tell precisely what this expression means to say, *i.e.,* that *metanoias* here qualifies the *bap.,* tells what kind of a *bap.* it is—that the chief, true, real characteristic of it is this *metanoia*—that it proceeds from, rests upon it, involves it—as its cause, motive, value, justification. Read everything in connection with John's baptism—historically, doctrinally, ethically—and you will see this with absolute certainty and clearness. I need not indicate this to you. John's great mission was to preach repentance; he would not receive to his baptism those who had not repented, or those of whose repentance he was not assured as genuine. Note his directions to the various classes who came to him, and asked what they were to do to testify to the reality of their *metanoia.*

"If we could manipulate our English tongue in the construction of compounds, as the Germans do theirs, we would call this baptism a *repentance* baptism. The Germans call it a *Buss-Taufe;* that would show the precise relation of repentance to baptism in this case. Many, very many, such cases of the use of the genitive occur in Greek, and in the Greek New Testament, as well as in the Septuagint, or in the Hebrew Scriptures similarly. Let me note a few:—*to pneuma tes aletheias,* 'the spirit of truth;' John cc.: 14 and 15, and I John 4:6; *to pneuma tes planes, ib; basileus dikaiosunes.* Winer regards such expressions as *nomos tou andros,* Rom. 7:2; *nomos tou leprouy* Lev. 14:2; *Soma tes sarkosy* Col. 1:22; *{en to somatites sarkos')*—*i.e.,* the body in which carnality permanently dwells, as illustrations of this use of the genitive— as 'qualifying, characteristic.' To this may be added *soma tes hamartias; i.e.,* the body which belongs to sin, and in which sin dwells; which sin characterizes."

1.   "The question concerning *'eis aphesin hamartion'* is, I think, a very simple one. So far as the preposition *eis* is concerned, its natural, general force is perfectly well understood—that it denotes relation in the way of motion or tendency towards, or to, or into an object—the second two being the *full* expression of the idea. This notion of relation is, however, naturally variable, since the relation has, necessarily, many modifications, even in the physical sense. To intelligent minds this needs no argument or illustration; it is so with all words of this sort.

"Then, in the sense not physical, when it denotes mental action, in the relations of things not material— again many modifications must arise. This is all so plain that it must be accepted without debate.

"We cannot, in this case, as in many other cases, at once decide, from the mere presence of the preposition, that it denotes *for,* unto, into; *i. c.,* 'to reach, or attain to'—the forgiveness of sins. But, most certainly, from the nature of the preposition and the form of the statement in the text, *this* is the meaning that would' at once easily and promptly be suggested to the mind—to be maintained unless some strong reason arising, necessarily and imperatively, from the nature of the case, should oblige us to modify it—in other words, the burden of proof that it does not mean *for, i. e.,* 'to attain to, ' lies certainly and heavily on him who denies this simple, primary, obvious sense of the preposition and expression. I think no scholarly unprejudiced man will deny this; it is too plain.

2. "The expression, *'eis aphesin hamartion'* is, fortunately, not limited to the history of John's baptism, as given by Mark and Luke. Suppose we allow that this occurrence of these words needs further light to determine certainly its exact meaning; we can refer at once to a recurrence of these words where no question can possibly arise about its definite import. Math. 26:28. Who doubts, who questions that the blood of Jesus the blood of the New Covenant—is *for,* brings to the remission. Without the shedding of blood there is no remission of sins, is the Divine Law. Heb. 2:22.

"This process of determining the meaning of these words relative to John's baptism is strictly according to accepted laws of exegesis, and the only just and safe one.

"Finally, with impartial and competent expounders, men who could address themselves to this task with the necessary ability of scholarship, scriptural knowledge, and exegetical skill and freedom from creed-bias, there has been no trouble about the meaning of these words, declarative of the character and purpose of the baptism of John.

"There has been, also, a very remarkable unanimity in the great current of the mind and judgment of the Church from the beginning down the ages including the apostolic period and that of the fathers, when the language of the New Testament was yet the language of the great Eastern Church. It is only religious prepossessions that have made what is so singularly simple and clear, the ground of obscurity, doubt, and controversy—most unnecessarily and perversely so. When I say preversely, I do not mean in actual intention, but in fact.

"I hope this will be satisfactory. I have striven to be brief, simple, and plain.

"Affectionately, your brother,

"Chas. Louis Loos.
Lexington, Ky., *May* 19, 1891."

Greek-English Lexicon of the New Testament, being Grim's Wilke's "Clavis Novi Testimenti," Translated, Revised, and Enlarged by Joseph Thayer, D. D., says:

"*Eis,* a prep, governing the accusative and denoting entrance into, or direction and limit into, to, towards, for, among. It is used, A. Properly, 1. Of place, after verbs of going, coming, sailing, flying, falling, living, leading, carrying, throwing, sending, etc.; of a place entered, or of entrance into a place, into; and *(ci),* it stands before nouns designating an open place, a hollow thing, or one in which an object can be hidden; as, *eis* tan polin, etc. ... *(d) eis* means among *(in among)* before nouns comprising a multitude; as, *eis tons leestas;* Luke 10:36. ... If the surface only of the place is touched or occupied, *cis,* like the latin *in* may [often] be rendered on, upon, [sometimes] by unto (idioms vary), to mark the limit reached, or where one sets foot. Of this sort are *eis to per an.* Matt. 8:18, etc. ... of motion (not into a place itself, but) into the vicinity of a place, where it may be rendered *to near, towards* as, *"eis thalassan"* ... *"eis polin."* Mark 3:7, etc. ... II. of time; It denotes entrance into a period which is penetrated, as it were, *i.e.,* duration, *through a time ...; eis ton aioona,* and the like ... of the time in which a thing is done; because he who does or experiences a thing at any time is conceived of as, so to speak, entering into that time: ... B. used metaphorically, eis retains the force of entering into anything; where one thing is said to be changed into another, or to be separated into parts, or where several persons or things are said to be collected or combined into one, etc." ... I have omitted some of the minor subdivisions and most of the references. It should be noted that Thayer *defines eis* by the words: "denoting entrance into, or direction and limit: into, to, towards, for, among." His next words are: "It is used," etc. What follows is to show how the word *eis* is *used,* with citations, etc.

Section 11.

Chapter 1.
John 3:5

"Verily, verily, I say unto thee, Except a man be born of water and the Spirit, he cannot enter into the kingdom of God." In this passage I find what I suppose to be an allusion to the law of citizenship in the, then near at hand, Kingdom of Jesus Christ. Nicodemus came to Jesus by night and said: "Rabbi, we know that you are a teacher come from God, for no one can do these miracles that you do except God be with him." Having expressed his belief that Jesus was from God and that God was with him, Nicodemus proceeds, I suppose, to enquire of the great teacher the nature of the kingdom "near at hand," of which he had spoken, and to ask for the conditions on which he would be allowed to enter into it and to share its blessings. To this supposed enquiry Jesus replied: "Verily, verily, I say to you, Except one be born again he cannot see the kingdom of God." This being born again Nicodemus did not understand. He evidently thought, as his reply shows, that Jesus required him to be re-born, in the literal sense of the word. This, he conceived to be impossible. Especially did he think it strange that *he* should be required to be born again. He was, no doubt, honorably connected by birth, by virtue of which fact he then enjoyed senatorial honors. Why, then, should *he* be required to be born again?

Supposing it to be settled that he must be born again, the second part of his question is answered as follows: "Except one be born of water and spirit he cannot enter into the kingdom of God." As Jesus says that in the absence of these specified conditions one cannot enter into the kingdom of God, I feel bound to think and to say that no one is able to enter into the kingdom of God who lacks them, or either of them. What, then, 1. is it to be "born of water and spirit"; and, 2. What are the blessings assured to him who is in this kingdom?

If this passage be an allusion to the law of naturalization into the kingdom of God, as I suppose it certainly is, then, since an allusion to a law must be explained or understood by the law itself, just as a figure is always to be understood by reference to the fact alluded to in the figure, so it follows that if there be any obscurity about this allusion it must all become plain by referring to the law. We have the law, as follows, in Matt. 28:19: "Go ye, therefore, and make disciples of all the nations, baptizing them into the name of the Father and of the Son and of the Holy Spirit;" and, Mark 16:16: "Go ye into all the world, and preach the gospel to the whole creation. He that believeth and is baptized, shall be saved;" and Luke: 24:47: "Thus it is written that the Christ should suffer and rise again from the dead the third day; and that repentance and remission of sins should be preached in his name among all the nations, beginning from Jerusalem."

Assuming that what, and all that each one of these records has in it is true, which we must of course do, it follows that the law in question required, and now requires, that the alien sinner should believe and repent and be baptized in order to be saved. Now, as the *saved,* and they only, are those who are to be admitted into the kingdom of God, it seems to follow that those and only those who comply with this law, are in the kingdom of God. But Jesus says that the one born of water and spirit is the *only one* who is or can be in the kingdom of God. So to be born of water and spirit is equal to believing and repenting and being baptized.

It is known to all Greek scholars that the Greek word, here used and translated born, signifies to beget, as well. Therefore, in translating its more than one hundred occurrences in the New Testament, if from the connection, it is seen that fatherhood is the idea it is *beget,* generation, etc., but if the idea be that of motherhood, born, etc., is the translation. Again, if the idea intended to be conveyed be, not to distinguish between these two conceptions but rather to declare the consummation of both, the word should be rendered born; for, to say of one, he is born, is to say implicitly that he has been begotten.

In John 3:5, the word should be rendered *born,* since the entire process or the consummation of *all that* the word signifies is declared. If the word should be employed of God, of the spirit of God, of an apostle of God, or of the word of God, the translation should be *beget,* begotten, etc.

What is the meaning of the phrase: "born of the spirit?" This question is answered by this same apostle John in I. John 5:1: "Whosoever believeth that Jesus is the Christ *is begotten* of God. To be begotten of God, and to be begotten by the spirit of God is, of course, the same thing. Therefore, the above quotation informs us that the spiritual status of the one begotten of the Spirit is that he has believed, or he is a believer. Hence, to be begotten or born of the Spirit is to believe. Jesus says: "He that believeth and is baptized shall be saved."

But we have seen that to be begotten of the Spirit is to believe. And we have said that to be saved is substantially or practically the equivalent of being in the kingdom of God. Now, in the law we have the term baptism, and in the *allusion* to the law, we have the phrase, "born of water." To what does this phrase in the allusion correspond in the law? There is but one thing left to which it could allude, and that is baptism. To be born of water is, then, to be baptized. To sum up the correspondences between the allusion and the law, now pointed out, we have:

- To be begotten of the spirit is equal to believing.
- To be born of water is equal to being baptized.
- To be in the kingdom of God is equal to being saved.

As Jesus says: No one is able to enter into the kingdom of

God, except he be born of water and spirit; so, unless one believes and is baptized he cannot enter into the kingdom of God.

This conclusion is not even doubtful, provided the phrase, "born of water," is equivalent to, or signifies baptism. I think it is certain that Jesus meant by it, baptism, provided the word *water* is to be taken to signify, literally, water, for water is not present in any institution or ceremony of the Christian religion or church, except in baptism.

The fact that a word *may be* employed in a figurative sense is not by any means to be taken as proof that *this* word is so employed in *this passage.* The presumption is always against a figurative sense. Therefore, he who asserts a figurative use of the word, in this passage, must prove it, else judgment must go against him. Can one prove it? Only a very few persons, of thousands, have ever so affirmed; and no one, even of these, so far as I have been able to find, has ever made a *serious effort to prove it.*

Suppose one should undertake to prove that the word water (Greek, hudor) in John 3:5, does not mean water, but something else, how must he proceed? I suppose he must say that the word does necessarily have its plain current sense—water—in this passage, unless the sense of the connection or some fact or truth in the document of which it is a part does absolutely forbid it. But there is no such forbidding sense in the connection; nor is there any fact or truth in the document opposed to the current sense of the word.

Is there any impossibility or incongruity in the idea of being born of water? I see none. Indeed, the birth of water is so like to a literal birth, that the use of the metaphor is most reasonable and striking. If one should be unable to see the likeness or to justify the use of the figurative expression, "born of water," I would call his attention to the fact that the rising out of the grave is called, by the spirit of God, a birth. See Col. 1:18: "And he is the head of the body, the Church, who is a beginning, a first-born (ek ton nekron) from among the dead." See, also, Rev. i: 5: "and from Jesus Christ, the faithful witness, the first-born of the dead." The Greek word for born in these two quotations is tikto, which never signifies to *beget,* but always, to give birth, or its equivalent. To be born of water is certainly as rational and defensible a statement as to be born of the grave. But the latter statement is gladly accepted and never by Christians denied; so the former ought not to be denied.

Assuming now, as I think I may, that the Greek word here signifies water, it follows that to be "born of water" is to be baptized. It also follows from the premises before us, that, unless one is baptized he cannot enter into the kingdom of God. And as to enter into the kingdom of God is practically the equivalent of the forgiveness of sins, it follows that baptism is a condition of remission of sins, or is for the remission of sins.

But, for the purpose of, if possible, a still higher degree of assurance, I will cite the opinions of several persons and parties, viz.: "Alford's Greek Testament," page 643, "There can be no doubt, on any honest interpretation of the words, that *'born* of water' *(Genne thanai ex hudatos)* refers to the token or outward sign of baptism—*ek pneumatos* to the thing signified, or inward grace of the Holy Spirit. All attempts to get rid of *these two plain facts* have sprung from doctrinal prejudices, by which the views of expositors have been warped."

Alford thinks *there can be no doubt* but that *doctrinal prejudices,* by which expositors have been *warped,* explain how anyone could interpret the "plain words, born of water," otherwise than as referring to water baptism. Any other interpretation, he supposes, is hardly an honest one. When we come to consider the character and standing of this witness, and the unequivocal* character and dogmatic style of his testimony, it is not easy to see how any greater assurance could be had from any uninspired testimony.

Again, as proof that water baptism is to be understood by the phrase, "born of water," in this verse, I read from Dr. Wall, "History of Infant Baptism," Vol. I., 43. I quote from the Oxford edition, University press, 1862: "And thirdly, because we see by it that they understood that rule of our Savior, *Except one be regenerated* (or born again) of water and the *Spirit, he cannot enter into the kingdom of God,* of water baptism; ... And so did all the writers of these 400 years, not one man excepted." At this point Wall is commenting upon the writings of Justin Martyr, who wrote about the middle of the 2nd century. On the high authority of Dr. Wall we are assured that for 400 years of the first years of Christianity *not* one man denied that "born of water," signified water baptism.

On page 92, same vol., in commenting on the writings of Cyprian, and in regard to the words, *born of water,* Dr. Wall says: "There is not any one Christian writer of any antiquity, in any language, but what understands it of baptism. And if it be not so understood, it is difficult to give an account how a person is born of water any more than born of wood." This is plain and stands as a historical statement unchallenged since the days of Justin Martyr, A. D. 140, till, comparatively, but a few years ago. There is, perhaps, no important text of the scriptures in regard to which there has been so little dispute as in regard to the phrase, "born of water," in John 3:5, until quite recently. And even since opposition to the plain sense of the passage has come up, it has been, as Dr. Wall says: on account of doctrinal prejudices of commentators, expositors, etc. It looks as though, in the light of such testimony, nothing further need be said. But to the testimony now before us on this point, I add as follows: Bengel says, "born of water" means baptism; Moses Stuart says it means baptism; Albert Barnes says the same; John Wesley says it means baptism; Bloomfield says the same; The Methodist Discipline takes the same view; the Presbyterian Confession of faith quotes it as signifying baptism, and so does the Episcopal prayer-book. If the citation of authorities may be allowed to establish, as correct, an interpretation of a scripture, the meaning of this passage is settled by the foregoing, especially as it should, and may be truthfully added that this list of illustrious names might be easily increased to many hundreds, with but few and feeble dissenters of very recent date.

Assuming now, as may most certainly be done, that "born of water," means water baptism, and that it is an allusion to the baptism of the great commission, and that Nicodemus was enquiring for the conditions of admission into the kingdom, then near at hand, and of the enjoyment of the blessings thereof, a few concluding words will suffice to show the value of baptism, our objective point.

Jesus says: "Except one be born of water and spirit he cannot enter into the kingdom of God." That which stands between the sinner and the kingdom of God is the sins of the sinner; and those things which he must do before he *can enter* the kingdom of God are for the remission of his sins.

Whatever things one must do in order to get into the kingdom of God are, practically, the things he must do in order to the remission of his sins; or, whatever one must do to get into the kingdom of God, *is for the remission* of his sins. But the Savior says, *and it must be true,* as before explained, that, except one be born of water—*baptized*—and born of the spirit (believes) he cannot enter into the kingdom of God. Therefore, to be baptized is a condition of going into the kingdom of God. Hence, to be baptized is a condition of remission of sins, Q. E. D.

Does one ask: Why, in this allusion, is the water (baptism) put *before* birth of the spirit (belief)? I suppose this to be the explanation: The whole matter of conversation was as to *being in the kingdom of God.* Looked at from the standpoint of one going towards the kingdom but who is not in it, faith (born of the spirit) is seen and met with before baptism (born of water) is. But contemplating the matter from the standpoint of the kingdom and looking back, the order as thus seen and met, is reversed. This may be the true explanation of the facts in this case; I am not sure that it is, however.

Chapter 2.
Mark 16:9–20:

"Now when he was risen early on the first day of the week, he appeared first to Mary Magdalene, from whom he had cast out seven devils. She went and told them that had been with him, as they mourned and wept. And they, when they heard that he was alive, and had been seen of her, disbelieved. And after these things he was manifested in another form unto two of them, as they walked, on their way into the country. And they went away and told it unto the rest: neither believed they them. And afterward he was manifested unto the eleven themselves as they sat at meat; and he upbraided them with their unbelief and hardness of heart, because they believed not them which had seen him after he was risen. And he said unto them, Go ye into all the world, and preach the gospel to the whole creation. He that believeth and is baptized shall be saved; but he that disbelieveth shall be condemned. And these signs shall follow them that believe: in my name shall they cast out devils; they shall speak with new tongues; they shall take up serpents, and if they drink any deadly thing, it shall in no wise hurt them; they shall lay hands on the sick, and they shall recover. So then the Lord Jesus, after he had spoken unto them, was received up into heaven, and sat down at the right hand of God. And they went forth, and preached everywhere, the Lord working with them, and confirming the word by the signs that followed. Amen."

I. It would not be right that I should use these verses as important evidence in support of my position without submitting that their genuineness is called in question by some critics of the highest authority.

I find in the commentary on Mark 16:9–20, by Prof. McGarvey, of the Bible College, Kentucky University, what, with a few additional statements, will be sufficient for our purpose in this work. I quote as follows:

> Let it be first observed that it is not the authenticity of the passage by which is meant the historical correctness of its representations that is called in question, but only its genuineness as a part of Mark's original manuscript. A few remarks on its authenticity, however, will not, at this point, be out of place.
>
> All the historical statements of the passage are known to be true, independently of their occurrence here, because they are found in the gospels or in Acts. Thus the statements concerning the appearance of Jesus to Mary Magdalene, which occupy verses 9–11, are substantially verified by John and Luke. (See John 20:1—18; Luke 8:2, and compare the notes on Mark 16:9–11.) The statement concerning his appearance to two disciples as they went into the country, is but a brief account of what is more fully described in Luke 24:13–35, and yet it is so varied in expression as to show that it is not an abbreviation from Luke. (See the note on 16:12, 13.) All the items of the appearance of Jesus to the eleven, described in verse 14, are substantiated by the statements in Luke 24:36–43, and John 20:19–23; and those pertaining to the commission and the ascension (15, 16, 19, 20), are confirmed by Luke's account of the latter (24:36–51), and by Matthew's report of the former (28:19–20); while the promise concerning the signs that were to follow the believers is substantially included in Matt. 28:20, and John 14:12, and is fully verified by the events recorded in Acts.
>
> Not only are the statements of the passage thus proved to be authentic, but the manner in which the details are handled, and the forms of expression employed, show unmistakable marks of an original writer. His

sources of information were independent of the narratives of Matthew, Mark, Luke, and John, and yet they were correct. He must, then, have lived and written previous to the general circulation of the other gospels, and within II the apostolic age. This is conceded by Alford, who is one of the most confident writers in opposition to the genuineness of the passage. He says: "The inference, therefore, seems to be that it is an authentic fragment placed as a completion of the gospel in very early times; by whom written, must, of course, remain wholly uncertain; but coming to us with very weighty sanction, and having strong claims on our reception and reverence." (Com. Mark, 16:9, 20.)

The authenticity of the passage being conceded, and the fact being apparent that it was written by someone possessed of independent and correct sources of information, the question of its genuineness might be waived without detracting from its authority or credibility; for, a true piece of history attached to Mark's book is not less valuable or authoritative because some other person than Mark may have been the author of it; but we proceed, for the sake of a thorough understanding of the facts in the case, to examine the evidence *pro* and *con,* and first those which are called external evidences:

First, the manuscripts. The passage is omitted from a few of the manuscripts, and among these are the Vatican and Sinaitic, the two oldest and best manuscripts extant. ... Jerome, and some writers of the fourth century, are also quoted as. affirming that the passage was wanting in most of the Greek copies of their day.

On the other hand, the passage is found in nealy all of the other ancient manuscripts, including the Alexandrian, which stands next to the Vatican in accuracy. It was also cited by Irenaeus and Tatian of the second century, and by Hyppolytus and Dyonisius of Alexandria, of the third century, all of whom lived before the earliest existing manuscript was written, and from one hundred to two hundred years earlier than-Jerome. The words of Irenaeus show that it was not only a part of the book of Mark in his day, but that Mark was regarded as its author. He says: "But Mark, in the end of his gospel, says, 'And the Lord Jesus, after that he had spoken to them, was received up into heaven, and sat at the right hand of God.' From these writers, then, it appears that the passage was a part of Mark's gospel at least as early as the second century. The preponderance of evidence from this source is in favor of the passage.

Second, the ancient versions. The evidence from this source is altogether in favor of the passage; for, all the ancient versions contain it, and thereby testify that it was in the Greek copies from which they were translated. If, at this time, the Greek copies did not generally contain it, it is, at least, a very remarkable circumstance that all the versions were made from those that did. Among these versions are the Peshito Syriac, the Old Italic, the Sahidic, and the Coptic, all of which were in existence earlier than the Sinaitic and Vatican manuscripts, and before the time of Jerome.

Third, critical conjecture. The relative probability of the passage having been written by Mark or added by a later hand, is next to be considered. Those who adopt the latter hypothesis think that the addition was made on account of the want of completeness apparent in closing the narrative with the eighth verse of this chapter. Any reader will be struck with this want of completeness, if he will read from the first to the eighth verse, and imagine that the narrative there closes. But while this consideration would account for the addition of the passage, it leaves unaccounted for the fact that Mark cut short his narrative so abruptly. The various conjectures advanced to account for this fact, such as the sudden death of Mark, or the sudden death of Peter,

Mark's instructor; are so unsatisfactory that they serve only to show the strait in which the writers find themselves who adopt this hypothesis. On the other hand, if we suppose that the passage was written by Mark, its absence from some copies is at once accounted for by considering the many accidents by which the last leaf of a manuscript may be lost. Alford himself recognizes the force of this consideration, and says, 'The most probable supposition is that the last leaf of the original gospel was torn away.' This remark of his is intended by him to account for the incompleteness which suggested the addition of the passage in question, but we think it still more satisfactorily accounts for the absence of this passage from those manuscripts which have it not; for one manuscript with the last leaf torn away, or worn away, might be used as a copy, and might thus become the prolific mother of an immense brood of manuscripts lacking the portion lost.

As regards the external evidence, then, we are constrained to adopt the conclusion of Dr. Davidson, who very modestly says: 'On the whole, the external arguments in favor of the passage outweigh those on the other side.' (Davidson's Introduction.)

We believe that, in this conclusion, *all the critics concur,* and that the ground of doubt which overrules it, in the minds of some, is internal evidence furnished by words and phrases found in the passage which are foreign, it is claimed, to Mark's style, and which, therefore, show the hand of another writer."

Thus deposes Prof. McGarvey, who is one of the most competent, patient, and painstaking critics known to me. Following this, and in the same article, the Professor examines the question, whether the words and phrases of the passage do in fact furnish internal evidence against the genuineness or authenticity of it. This part of his argument is learned, lengthy, and somewhat difficult to be understood by the common reader. At the conclusion he says:

> "Our final conclusion is that the passage in question is authentic in all its details, and there is no reason to doubt that it was written by the same hand which indicted the preceding parts of this narrative. The objections which have been raised against it are better calculated to shake our confidence in Biblical Criticism than in the genuineness of this inestimable portion of the word of God."

The most weighty and the latest objections to the genuineness of the passage in question are found in the "Introduction to New Testament, Appendix I., page 51," by Westcott and Hort. I quote from "The Text and the Canon," by Prof. McGarvey, page 16: "There is no difficulty in supposing that the true intended continuation of verses 1–8 either was very early lost by the detachment of a leaf or was never written down; and that a scribe or editor, unwilling to change the words of the text before him, or to add words of his own, was willing to furnish the gospel with what seemed a worthy conclusion by incorporating with it, unchanged, a narrative of Christ's appearances after the resurrection, which he found in some secondary record then surviving from the preceding generation. If these suppositions are made, the whole tenor of the evidence becomes clear and harmonious. Every other view is, we believe, untenable." It is herein seen that these distinguished critics deny that Mark is, directly, the author of the disputed passage. But they seem to allow that the statements of the passage are true and authoritative, therefore. Alford, who also denies that Mark is the real author, still asserts that the verses are an "authentic fragment." I have, herein, brought prominently forward the strongest objections that can be marshalled against the passage, and yet it is seen that even these hold the opinion that the *truth* of the statements in question may not be, reasonably, denied. There is, I believe, no valid reason to doubt that Mark 16:9–20, is, in every important feature and particular, "the word of God."

I do not give names and quotations on the other side, for the reason that the number of the names, very distinguished, and the sum of their pertinent statements to our purpose, are too great. The critical examination of this question belongs elsewhere. I have aimed only to say what would make it quite apparent that I might, and should of right, use the lessons of this scripture in the course of my argument.

Chapter 3.
The Great Commission Taught and Practiced

Mark 16:16. This passage reads: "One, having believed and having been baptized, shall be saved; but one having not believed, shall be condemned." Or: "He that has believed and has been baptized, shall be saved; but he that has believed not shall be condemned." Each of these translations is true to the original. In the former, I give the aorist participle its true representative in English, *as a participle;* in the latter, I give the participle its tense signification, but translate it as a finite verb, for which good authority gives permission.

The meaning of the words of this passage, taken with the grammatical force of the construction, are an answer to the question: Who shall be saved? The one who asks the question is supposed to be lost, to want to know what to do to be saved and to have some degree of confidence in the one to whom he puts the question. Hence, in the answer to the supposed question, the verb declaring the salvation of the enquirer should be, as it respects him, in the future tense; and so it is. But, from the standpoint of the man in a state of salvation, the things that one must do in order to be saved must have already occurred; hence, the participles by which the things that were done are expressed, should be in the definite past tense, and so they are. These facts ought to appear in the translation. The first thing in time and in importance when attempting to ascertain what one means is to find precisely what he says. What Jesus really said, is, I believe, fully and definitely expressed in the above rendering; and it must be allowed that he said just what he meant to say, and that he meant what he said. He said that the one who would be saved, must, in order to be saved, looked at from the salvation point, have believed and have been baptized.

To be saved is, I presume, to be pardoned, or, to obtain remission of sins. This is so obviously true that I do not attempt to prove it. Now, substituting the phrase: *"remission of sins"* for *" saved* the Savior's language would be: If one would obtain remission of sins he must believe and be baptized. Or, if one has remission of sins he must have believed and have been baptized. So, believing and being baptized, tied together by the conjunction, *and,* are therefore, in the great commission, declared to be in order to being saved or having remission of sins. Therefore, baptism is for "remission of sins," q. e. d.

Whether one may be saved without doing these things, no heart, loyal to Jesus Christ, is very careful to know. I am not, herein, attempting to answer such a question. It is quite enough for us to know what the Divine requirement for salvation is and to do it, leaving in the hands of God, *as we must,* the solution of the question whether one may be saved, having omitted to believe and to be baptized, or either of them.

In the latter part of the verse Jesus gives, not the conditions of salvation, but of condemnation. So, should one desire to know the condition of condemnation, he has it, plainly stated: He that believeth not shall be condemned. That is, as long as it is true of one that he has not believed, it is true that he shall be condemned. I see no reason for translating *apisteusan,* disbelieves, or, having disbelieved. The word simply means, to not believe. The translation, *disbelieve,* found in "the revision," and in some other excellent versions, I suppose, comes of the fact that the authors wished to leave the way open for the salvation of infants and certain other parties. But the way for the salvation of infants, etc., is quite wide open without this unnecessary strain being put upon the word of God.

When God says that if one does not believe he shall be condemned, He is not talking to nor of an infant, nor of any one not accountable before the law. The translation which I make is offered solely on the ground of fidelity to the original and not at all because the old version or any translation known to me is in the least out of harmony with the doctrine I am advocating. It has been said that the latter part of the verse does not say: "and is not baptized," shall be damned, and the supposed conclusion from this fact is that not being baptized would not be a ground of condemnation; and that it follows that baptism is not a condition of remission of sins. To say, in reply to this, anything to one who does not care to *reason* would be labor lost; to say very much to a thoughtful, anxious investigator for truth would be unnecessary; for, one who does not believe is condemned already, no matter what else may or may not be true. Moreover, such an one cannot be baptized if he would, and, if he be honest, he cannot *'wish to be baptized,* if he could be. Hence, in reason and according to the Bible, the case of anyone who does not believe is, if responsible for the exercise of faith, already closed. He, being an unbeliever, no matter what baptism is for, is condemned, and there is no reason for saying: "and is not baptized."

But suppose Jesus had said: He that believeth not and is not baptized, shall be condemned. Well, in that case, if one should believe but should not be baptized, he, of course, could not be lost. Or, if one should believe not, but should be baptized, he could not be lost. Such one could not stay here always, and, as we have seen, that he can neither go to heaven nor to perdition, what is to become of him?

Those who make this, so called, criticism are, I fear, more inclined to dictate to the Divine Father than they are to be taught by him; more disposed to have their own will than to pray, "thy will be done, not mine." I do not believe that more than one in a thousand persons, who *wish* to be saved, who are not seeking a short or easy way to heaven, who are ready to deny self and allow that God shall . be all in all, and who look at this great commission in its wonderful plainness with a single eye, would hesitate for a moment to accept, substantially, the view that I have here taken.

As additional evidence that this record in Mark 16 is an authentic deliverance from God, in substance at least, if not in form; and that its lesson is correctly stated in the foregoing, I cite and comment on: Matt. 28:19: "Go (or going), disciple all the nations, baptizing them into the name of the Father and of the Son and of the Holy Spirit, teaching them to observe all things whatever I have commanded you." This translation will, I doubt not, be accepted as correct.

I next enquire: What does the passage mean? As the meaning of a sentence is known by ascertain ing the meaning of its words, let us enquire: What is the meaning of some of the leading words in this record of the commission?

1.   Disciple *{Matheteuo).* The noun of the family is mathetes, a disciple or learner under a master or teacher. *Mathetes* is from *Manthano,* to learn. The verb, matheteuo, to make disciples, has in it the idea of teaching—the means of disciplining and learning—and also the result of the teaching and learning—that is, becoming a pupil or disciple.

In this commission the Lord charges the apostles to so operate upon "the nations" as to bring as many as possible into the school of the Christ, the great Teacher. In doing this work, they, of course, were not to employ any force or influence other than what is in the instructions which they imparted, and the motives which they employed to induce the people of the nations to accept of the offer of salvation through Jesus Christ.

Plainly, they were *to teach* and *to persuade* the people to become the pupils of Jesus. The old translation, in this place, is not a bad one. It tells a large part of what the apostles were to do in making disciples. They were to teach. The word *teach* does not, however, carry forward the thought, necessarily, so far as to result in, or to contemplate, the idea of the taught becoming pupils in the school; whereas the word *disciple* does.

One may be taught the doctrine of Christ and not be or become what Jesus demanded. Therefore the word teach is inadequate to convey the idea that Jesus had. But the word *disciple* pointed to the full measure of apostolic duty in the premises and demanded of the nations what Jesus wished and what they needed. The word used looked to the consummation of the work commanded. So, according to Matthew, the apostles were expected, when disciplining persons, to teach, to convince them of the duty and necessity of, intelligently, entering into the school of Christ, and to persuade them, if possible, to do so. Those who heard the apostles would not, and were not expected to, become disciples unless they should believe. So the discipling of Matthew is the complement of the believing of Mark. Therefore, the record of Mark is true, whatever else may be said of it.

2. *Them.* Matthew says: "Baptizing *them.*" *Autous,* them, is a pronoun, and it seems to stand for the noun, nations (ethne). But it does not. The word *ethne,* nations, is neuter gender, whereas the pronoun *(autous')* them, is masculine gender. This fact indicates that the pronoun, them, does not, probably, stand for or represent, strictly, the word nations. It suggests that, though effort should be made by teaching, etc., to induce *all* the people of the nations to come to Christ or to enlist in his school, yet that *not all* were, necessarily, to be baptized. If it had been designed that *all* to whom preaching was to be done were to be baptized, the pronoun showing who were to be baptized would have been of the same gender as the noun "nations." But this is not the case. From this it is clear that the *ethne,* nations, as such,

were not to be baptized, but that such part of the people as might be represented by the pronoun *them,* having some noun of the masculine gender as its antecedent, might be and should be. This noun is not *expressed* in the connection but it is plainly implied. It is present in sense. The common sense of the passage is, that when the apostles preached to the people, if they should believe, or accept the teachings, or should be discipled, then they (the disciples) should be baptized. That is, the apostles were to, if possible, make disciples of all the nations and baptize them, not all the nations, but only those whom they had discipled. They were to baptize the disciples.

The term, Mathetes, disciples, is, in Greek, masculine gender. To this term, present in sense, the pronoun *them,* refers, as its antecedent; and with it the pronoun agrees in gender, according to a rule of grammar that so requires.

For this conclusion I have the very best of authorities. I quote "Winer's Grammar of the Greek New Testament," section 24, page 141, 7th edition: "It is a peculiarity, common to the pronouns, whether personal, demonstrative, or relative, that they not infrequently take a different gender from that of the nouns to which they refer, regard being had to the *meaning* of the *nozins,* not to their grammatical sex. This is called *construct ad sensum,* the *meaning* and not the grammatical gender of the word being mainly considered. It is used particularly when some animate object is denoted by a neuter or an abstract feminine noun. The pronoun is then made to agree grammatically with the object in question."

After thus deposing, Winer proceeds to cite this particular passage in Matt. 28:19, as a case in point, under his rule. Thus it appears that, as Mark baptizes believers, Matt, baptizes disciples.

That *disciples* were to be baptized and not persons without mental and moral qualifications, may be inferred from the following: "As, therefore, the Lord knew that the Pharisees had heard that Jesus was making and baptizing more disciples than John," etc. John 4:1. This is what the Pharisees heard; but as there is no intimation that what they had heard was untrue, it is highly probable that those who were being baptized by the apostles under the eye of Jesus were discipled and then baptized. It is also clear that the discipling was not done by baptizing, for the text expressly says that he made disciples *and* baptized them.

It is safe to conclude that Mark's believers are the same as Matthew's disciples, and that the believing and being baptized of Mark is the discipling and baptizing of Matthew.

"Into the name," etc. It is here stated that the one discipled, was, when baptized, brought "into the name of the Father and of the Son and of the Holy Spirit." Our enquiry is, what does "into the name," mean?

That *eis* signifies *into,* and that it should be uniformly so rendered wherever the sense will permit, is not now a debatable question. Among scholars whose reason goes before *prejudice* and *wish,* whose principle is, *be slow, careful,* when dealing in and with Divine things, I believe I may say there is no such question. As I shall consider this Greek preposition more *fully* in another place, I shall say no more of it here. For the present I assume that *"eis* to onoma," the Greek of the phrase, signifies "into the name."

Israel is said, I. Cor. 10:2, to have been baptized into Moses, in the cloud and in the sea. As a fact they were not, literally, in Moses, yet they were in him; for, so the Divine record says. They were, then, in him, in a figurative sense. Moses' object, purpose, or business was to give the people salvation. God had sent, commissioned, and qualified him to do this for Israel. They listened to Moses; they decided to obey, to follow him; they did follow him to the Red Sea. Up to this time they were in their enemies' country; they were not yet delivered—saved. The steps thus far taken were necessary, were essential to, and they were in order to, their salvation from Egyptian bondage. But they were not yet saved. Their enemies were yet alive, and they were pursuing them with great vengeance and power. They murmured against Moses. They were not yet fully committed "into Moses." Moses commanded them to be baptized—to "go forward." They went into the sea, under the cloud. They came out of their baptism with gladness in their hearts and songs of *salvation* upon their lips. Ex. 15:1, *et seq.* They were now bound for the promised land, and were fully committed to, and were dependent upon Moses, and their enemies were destroyed in the sea where they had just been baptized. Their dependence was now so entirely in Moses, and their baptism in the cloud and sea being the final act of shutting off their enemies from them forever and of devoting them to Moses entirely, they are, therefore, said to have been "baptized into Moses." They, literally, were under the rule, guidance, or control of Moses.

It seems, then, that when the committal of their destiny to Moses was complete, and their dependence for salvation was, absolutely, in him, the formal and consummating act which brought to them that end, is said to have put them into Moses.

So, we are said to be baptized into Christ. Gal. 3:27; Rom. 6:3. This, of course, signifies the taking of him as our only authority, rule, or guide, our only dependence for salvation. All of our faith and hope center in him. Now, as baptism *consummated* that relation we are said to be baptized into him. A baptized one is, figuratively, in Jesus Christ, and in the literal sense he is in his government, under his control or guidance, in his kingdom. Just as the blessings promised to Israel were conditioned upon their being in Moses, in the sense herein explained, so the blessings promised to us through Jesus Christ are conditioned upon our being in him.

We are said to be baptized into the name of the Lord Jesus. Acts 8:16, and 19:5. To be baptized "into the name of the Lord Jesus," is, I doubt not, the same as to be baptized into Christ. In each case the literal fact is, we are actually inducted into the kingdom of God, and are made mete to be partakers of the inheritance of the Saints in light. It is expressly declared that God blesses us with *all* spiritual blessings, in heavenly places, *in Christ.* Gal. 1:3. And if one "be *in Christi* is a new creation." II. Cor. 5:17. It is not only shown in these passages *how* one comes into Christ, but it is also apparent what the character of one *in Christ* is, and what his blessings are; viz.: "He is a new creature;" all spiritual blessings in heavenly places are his; he has put on Christ; he is in his death with the hope of being saved. Indeed, the line which separates between those *"Christ"* and those not in Christ, is the line that divides the righteous from the wicked, the saved from the lost, the forgiven from those who are not forgiven. Of course, herein we are not speaking of the mere *ceremony* of baptism apart from the conditions of soul implied in the already possessed faith unfeigned and repentance in the heart. For, when so considered, *it is nothing;* indeed, it is not anything.

The attempt, if made, to have baptism by itself is an impertinence and vain. Yet, it is said, but said, of course, of those only who are ready—prepared—for the birth into the new life, that we are "baptized into Christ," and thus "put on Christ."

In the presence of such lessons from God, no one, it seems to me, who is seriously respectful and reverential, could speak lightly of being baptized, or could feel entirely comfortable while a cloud of doubt should hang over the question of fact whether one has been baptized or not.

Rom. 6:3, says: "Or, are you ignorant that we who were baptized into Christ Jesus were baptized into his death?" What does "baptized into his death" mean? In one case we are said to be baptized into Christ, then into Christ Jesus, then into the *name* of the Lord Jesus, now into his death. He "died for our sins, according to the scriptures." That is, in his death was opened, in the family of King David, "the fountain for sin," etc. It was the intention, no doubt, of the apostle to say that their baptism introduced them into the blessings, privileges, and honors of "*His* death." Jesus' blood was "shed for remission of sins." So, I repeat, baptized into his death signifies baptized into the benefits or blessings of his death. Among these blessings or benefits the chief is, remission of sins and such other blessings as ensue therefrom. Thus it seems to be certain that our baptism, when properly or scripturally fortified or qualified, brings us into a state of forgiveness of sins. Bu-t, Matthew says it brings us into the name of the Father and of the Son and of the Holy Spirit. Now, I conclude that the one who is brought *"into the name"* is the one who is brought into the Christ, into the body of Christ, into the death of Christ; is the one who has put on Christ, has reached the benefits of his sufferings and death, and has risen with him to walk in newness of life.

To be baptized *"into the name,"* then, is to come into the possession and enjoyment of all spiritual blessings in Christ Jesus our Lord. I believe this conclusion is fairly reached from the *facts* of the Holy Scriptures. With its proper antecedents, baptism into the *name,* etc., is for coming into Christ, into the death of Christ; is for putting on Christ; it is for, or in order to remission of sins. This being true, Mark's record, 16:9–20, is true or authentic; for it is, though in different words, the same as Matthew's record.

The Greek word, *"onoma"* signifies name. When John the Baptist was born his father said: His *"onoma"* (name) is John.

Names are given to designate or distinguish persons. Often, in the Bible, names are given to persons to designate them in respect to their profession, office, purpose, or business in life. This is true of Jesus Christ. He was called Jesus because he should save his people from their sins. His purpose or business in this world was to seek and save the lost. To be baptized into the name of Jesus Christ, was and is to be put or brought into the possession and enjoyment of the blessings of his mission or business in this world. To come into the name of one is to become so related to him as to, legally, inherit the blessings of his business, office, or purpose. If, under HIS own proclamation of salvation, persons are baptized into the *name* of Jesus Christ, the Son, and the Bible says they are, it is only a figurative way of saying that they are, through baptism, brought into the enjoyment of the blessings of his mission, or calling. Matthew's record of the great commission may, then, beyond doubt, be claimed as conclusively showing that Christian baptism is for remission of sins.

JESUS' MISSION.

Jesus, the great philanthropist, came into our world to seek and to save the lost. Were sinners looked upon as hungering, starving, dying? His kingdom was the offered refuge, and its provisions the remedy for all the ills of the soul. In this kingdom is safety, plenty, health, hope, happiness, life. All things pertaining to life and Godliness are found in unfailing abundance in Christ Jesus.

Salvation, as God contemplates it, is not confined to deliverance from sin. The blind, in heaven, see; the deaf hear; the dumb speak; the old have youth renewed like the eagles; all pains are gone; tears are wiped away; partings are no more; crying is no more; death is destroyed forever, is swallowed up in victory. Oh, the Saints shall cry, at the blessed consummation,—

"O death, where is thy sting;

O death, where is thy victory?"

As Jesus passed along to and fro, in his earth life, blessing kept even step with his going. The common people heard him, gladly. All said, Never did man speak as he. It was never so seen among men before. But his power and willingness to save from sin and give eternal life to men and women dead in trespasses and in sins, were the chief objects of his personal mission in the world. That he should, through his own death, destroy death — the last enemy—and bring out of the grave life and immortality to light, was and is the hard lesson to learn. And yet when this lesson is once learned it appears to be one of the simplest things, one of the most reasonable things, imaginable, that the hard heart and stubborn will of the sinner should be subdued by love. That the sinner might not have any ground for doubting the immeasurable greatness of God's love; that he might at once let the light and love of God into his soul, it is declared in the holy scriptures that God so loved the world that He gave His only begotten Son to die for us while we were yet sinners, in order that we, through his sufferings and death, might have life.

This love of God was exhibited before the eyes of men as it was seen in the sufferings and death of Jesus. The good news of salvation is essentially in and is bound up with the facts of the gospel—the death, the burial, and the resurrection of Jesus Christ. This gospel the apostles were given in charge to preach. When it is preached successfully to a sinner he is brought to see that he is a sinner, to see how great a wrong sin against God is; he is brought to see something of the length and breadth and height and depth of the love of God which is made to shine into and weigh upon his soul until he cries in agony of his spirit: Lord, what wilt thou have me to do? The answer to this question we have just learned from the great commission.

This commission is the "law of the spirit of life in Christ Jesus," that "made me free from the law of sin and of death.'' As sin is the sum of all spiritual evils, so this Divine and merciful prescription for sin is the sum of all remedies for sin. I have, in a few of the preceding pages, considered this gospel commission. I have supposed its language to be simple and very direct. I can conceive of no language more intelligible, more certainly unambiguous than that of the great commission. Keeping in mind that Jesus came to save those lost in sin, and that the road to this end lay along the way of Jesus' death, burial, and resurrection (I. Cor. 15:1–5), it is not hard to understand him when he said to his apostles, "Go ye into all the world and preach the gospel to the whole creation, He that has believed and has been baptized shall be saved." Every unsophisticated mind, looking at or listening to these plain words, would say that Jesus meant just what he said; meant that if one would be saved he should or must believe and be baptized. No question would, probably, arise in such a mind as to whether one might be saved though he should not do quite all that Jesus prescribed. Indeed, such an one, not purposing or wishing to fail, in the least, to do *all* that the Master called upon him to do, does not wish to know or to obtain an answer to that question. Duty is what he seeks, not *a bargain.* But plain as the language is, and improbable as it is that Jesus would, on so important a question as that of the salvation of the soul, use figurative or ambiguous language in giving us the *law of life,* it is true that good men do understand the commission as though it read: "He that has believed shall be saved, and he should be baptized." Strange as such a view of this language is *to me,* I must not, I do not speak of it otherwise than as the heart conviction of good, true men.

We have, then, the somewhat unusual case of very intelligent, educated, honest men who love God, differing as to the meaning of a scripture which certainly should be, and I think is as plain as any language in the word of God. We have tried to look carefully at the verbal, grammatical, and logical meaning and force of the language. The result is that Jesus seems to say that if one would be saved he should believe and (adding what Luke gives us in his record) repent and be baptized. As the object of giving this commission and of preaching the gospel was, and is, that all who believe it and repent of sins and are baptized shall receive remission of sins, it is manifest that each of the conditions stated by the law-giver is, in its place and in a measure, in order to remission of sins. No one of these expressed conditions is for remission of sins in the sense that it introduces one into remission of sins by virtue of its, alone, operation. Indeed, we have often said that there is *no virtue* in faith, repentance, confession, prayer, baptism, or *in any act* or *state* of *soul* or *body* to gain or secure the forgiveness of sins, except as such act or state has been prescribed or required by the word of God. Even then it is not the duty done that forgives the sins. It is God that justifies. Though I am concerned in this discussion only with the relation established between baptism and remission of sins, I have referred to other conditions that I might make it the more clear that I do not regard this ordinance as saving by its own operation or by itself; that there is no merit in the sinner nor in any act of his *for which* he *may claim forgiveness.* Salvation is by grace. It is God who forgives sins. It is manifest, however, that HE knows the characters to whom, and the conditions on which HE will bestow this great blessing, and that we do not, except as he has revealed them to us. What we claim is that God, in his revelation, has provided that those who would be saved, should believe, repent, and be baptized, assuring them that *thereupon (not therefor)* HE would forgive them.

But, as before stated, good men, true to their convictions of duty, learned men and wise, do not understand this commission, which is the guide and authority for the preacher, and the measure and designation of the duties of the sinner, as I do. This being true, it would not seem respectful in me to affirm, dogmatically, that I am right and that others, equally or more learned and pious, are wrong. Allowing, then, as I do, that it is at least possible that I am wrong in my conclusion as to the lessons of this great commission, let us, desiring more light, seek it with an humble and patient spirit.

Jesus gave the commission to the apostles who had been his disciples, or pupils in his school for three years and more, and who would, without the guidance of the Spirit, it would seem, understand Jesus' meaning. But, when to this it is added that these apostles were to tarry at Jerusalem till they should be endued with power from on high; that the power did come as promised, on the Pentecost; that the apostles were filled with the Holy Spirit and spake as the Spirit gave them utterance, it must be allowed that they understood, then, just what Jesus said and meant.

It is safe to say that the apostles, guided in every word and step by the infallible Spirit, taught just what Jesus commissioned them to teach; that they did just what Jesus commissioned them to do; that they required of the sinner just what and all that Jesus had bid them require; and that they promised the sinner just what the Master authorized them to promise him. In view of the commission under which they went forth, we would, reasonably, expect that the apostles, in bringing sinners to salvation here, and to the hope of eternal life hereafter, would preach to them the gospel, and that they would say, if sinners shall believe the gospel story, repent of their sins and be baptized they should be saved, and that all this is on the authority of Jesus Christ. This presumption arises logically out of the facts and accessories of the commission.

I now propose to examine the *"prax eis apostolon"*—the doings of the apostles—in which I am sure we shall see the commission, in the hands of these Divinely guided and therefore, infallibly right, agents of God, unfolded and applied. So, by observing what these ambassadors of the Christ taught and did, and required sinners to believe and do in order to be saved, we shall certainly come to understand the instructions which Jesus gave to his apostles, and, through them, gave to the world, for the salvation of sinners.

Acts 2:37, 38. This is the first *praxis*—act—of the apostles, under their commission. "The regeneration," here and now begins. The Church of Christ is now to be born. The apostles are "in Bank"—all together in one place—the power from on high has come upon them, and they begin the work of regeneration, speaking as the Spirit gave them utterance.

The evidence of THE SPIRIT'S presence and agency in what took place on this pentecost is seen, in the sound heard "as of the rushing of a mighty wind," in the "cloven tongues as of fire," and in the "speaking with tongues" which each of the apostles did as the Spirit gave them utterance. Under these inspiring and impressive circumstances the apostle Peter, full of the power of God, the wisdom of God and of the Spirit of God, that Jesus had said should guide the apostles into all truth, spoke. To him had been given the keys of the kingdom with which he is now about to open the door, that those prepared for it might enter into it. This was the first sermon preached under the great commission, and it was, of course, according to it. In view of the terms of his commission I would expect him to:

I. Preach the gospel. In doing this he must disabuse the minds of his hearers of any prejudices they might have against the apostles or against the cause which they were pleading, especially as to what they had just seen and heard. 2. He cites the prophecy of Joel, which they would, of course, and which many of them did, in fact, accept as of authority; and he declared that what they then saw and heard was the fulfillment of said prophecy. 3. He quoted David, saying, that David was a prophet, that as such he had foretold the resurrection of the Christ. The apostle announced that God raised up Jesus, of which fact, he said, "we all are witnesses." So Peter relied, for proof, upon the prophecies of Joel, the prophecies of David, the testimony of the apostles, and upon such facts as the hearers themselves knew. Thus the apostle endeavored to "let all the house of Israel know, assuredly, that God had made HIM both Lord and Christ—this Jesus, whom ye crucified." The argument was grand and logical as it was Divine and effectual. They heard that Jesus was to come according to the scriptures; that he did come to save sinners; that *they* had, themselves, been the betrayers and crucifiers of the innocent one who suffered that they might be saved; that he died, was buried, and that God had raised him from the dead, exalted him to His own right hand, and made him both Lord and Christ. "Now, when they heard *this* they were pricked in their heart, and said to Peter and the rest of the apostles, Brethren, what shall we do?" When pricked in their heart they had believed; for, so the expression signifies. They wished to know what they must do to be saved. It is obvious that, though they then believed, and that the facts, received in faith, had gone to their heart, and so they had what is sometimes called heartfelt faith, they did not regard themselves, as yet, saved. And the reply of Peter makes it too clear to allow of discussion that they were, indeed, not yet saved. The reason that they were not just then pardoned was, I suppose, because they had not yet come to the point where God could or had promised to forgive them. In the light of these facts it is clear that the point in their question was: what must we do *to be saved?* Peter was there, by the order of Jesus, for the express purpose of giving the desired information. He was there for the purpose of furnishing the infallibly correct answer to their question. What Peter did not say, in his answer, it is important in these days of irreverence for and departures from the word of God, to carefully note. It is not my purpose here, as it is not in the line of my argument to give any attention to this negative view. In his answer to their question the apostle said: "Repent, and let each one of you be baptized on the name of Jesus Christ, for forgiveness of sins." The Greek of this quotation is as follows: *"Metanoesate kai baptisthcto ekastos human epi to onomati Ie sou Christou eis aphesin hamartidn."* What the hearers had to do to be saved is here stated. They must repent and be baptized *for,* or in order to, or into, or unto, remission of sins. They had, as before stated, already believed. Therefore, Peter does not command them to believe; that is, to do what they had already done; but he requires them to do only what they yet lacked of having done, that they might be saved.

The commission under which he acted required him to say to sinners that they must believe and repent and be baptized. But as they had, on this occasion, already believed, but had not repented, nor been baptized, Peter would, must, and did command them to repent and be baptized.

The object which the hearers had in asking the question was that they might know what they must do to be saved. To be saved was to have their sins dismissed or sent away. To gain this end, now so intensely desired by them, Peter said that they must "repent and be baptized." These were the things which they had to do—those who had believed—and these are all that they had to do "for remission of sins." In view of these *obvious* facts, what was the design of their baptism? Can there be doubt on this point? The unprejudiced mind sees at once, sees clearly and does not doubt, that the repentance and the baptism were then and are now, "in order to remission of sins." So it seems to me. Unless what the apostle said in answer to their question, was to be *done in order to remission of sins,* the reply which he made was not an answer to their question at all. But it must be supposed that the apostle did answer their question, that he did announce to them the things they must do to be forgiven. Therefore, as before, "baptism is for remission of sins."

But, this reply of Peter's must, and must be understood' to, rest on a satisfactory foundation, not upon the wisdom or the authority of men.

Hence, the apostle assures his hearers that In pointing out their duty, in specifying the things they were to do, it all rested on the name of Jesus Christ.

The phrase, "on the name of Jesus Christ," in this passage, is for the purpose of declaring that the repentance and baptism were not human requirements or expedients, but that they rested, for validity and efficacy "on," as a foundation of assurance, the "name of Jesus Christ."

The word *name,* in this case, I believe, *stands* for authority and also for efficacy. So that, whatever of *authority* to require, or of *power* to guarantee to or confer blessings upon faithful obedient ones, there is in Jesus, is embraced in the phrase "in the name." That is, he who believes, repents, and is baptized, and does all of these in the service of and in submission to Jesus Christ, *with the whole heart,* in every act and deed, is assured by all that the prevailing name of Jesus Christ signifies, that he shall receive remission of sins.

Let us now look at the words *"eis aphesin hamartion,"* for remission of sins. "Aphesin hamartion," signify remission of sins; of this there is no doubt. Here there is no difference of opinion. If, now, we can determine the meaning of *eis* in the sentence, the purpose of repenting and of being baptized, as the apostle Peter required, becomes plain at once.

The preposition *"eis"* signifies *into.* This is its *current* meaning in the Greek New Testament. In this sense it must be received in all places where found, unless there is something in the context that absolutely forbids it. Even when the current meaning of a word is not admissible, the departure from this sense must be as small as possible. *Eis* is sometimes translated—by, to, unto, towards, in, for, in order to, etc.—and I do not say that all such renderings are inadmissible. Where circumstances so require, or necessity so compels, *eis* may be, probably, rendered *into* English by these words, or by most of them. But it should be noted, that, in all such cases, if there be such, and I think there are, the preposition has its real, full meaning shaded, obscured or limited. The translation, in such cases, is not that of *just* the word *eis,* but it is the meaning of *eis,* modified by the context.

Edward Robinson, D. D., in his lexicon of the Greek New Testament, says: *"eis,* a preposition, governing only the accusative, with the primary idea of motion into any place or thing, and then also of motion or direction *to, towards, upon,* any place or object. The antithesis is expressed by *ek, out of.* Septuagint everywhere for eis, See Winer, § 53, *a;* Mathews, § 578; Kiihner, § 290–2; Buttman, §147." After a lengthy and learned treatment the distinguished lexicographer says: ''Some times *eis* c. accus. is found where the natural construction would seem to require *en* c. dat; as after verbs which imply neither motion nor direction, but simply rest in a place or state. In such cases the idea of a previous *coming into* that place or state is either actually expressed or is implied in the context."

In so speaking, Dr. Robinson has only said what all lexicographers of note say. Besides his own valuable opinion, he gives us the names of Winer, Matthew, Kiihner, and Buttman, as sustaining him in it.

W. E. Jelf, D. D., "Grammar of New Testament Greek," vol. 2, p. 296, says of eis; "It expresses the same relations as *en* (in), except that it has the notion of a direction, *whither,* while *en* has the notion of rest, *where.* It is used to express the direction or motion of an action—*into* an object, or up to an object—into immediate contact with it, especially to express the reaching some definite point."

The foregoing quite fully shows that the preposition *eis,* which governs only the accusative, has for its primary notion the idea of "motion into any place or thing;" and also, it may be, "of motion or direction *to, towards, upon* any place or object," as Dr. Robinson says. To support this conclusion he cites Winer, Matthew, Kiihner, and Buttman. To these I add the names of Jelf, Stuart, *et al.* That is, I believe, all lexical and grammatical authorities hold the same view.

The purpose or objective point to be reached, or the end to be secured by the motion, which Dr. Robinson says is always expressed, or implied in the context, where *eis* is employed, is pointed out by the preposition *eis.* It takes up, as it were, the motion idea, expressed or implied, on the one hand, and points to the object or end which the movement is to reach, on the other. If it should be thought that the preposition is, in a few cases, so employed that the idea of motion is not quite apparent, still, Dr. Robinson thinks it is implied in the context. Even if this implication may not be allowed, still, all that can, by any means, be rationally claimed, is that an *exception to the rule is made out.* Where there is no *necessity* for departure from the rule of this preposition, of course no departure ought to be made. Add to the foregoing the fact that *eis* points out the objective point of the movement, which is expressed in the passage, or is implied in the context, as being *always after the movement,* and the conclusion is made as certain as any language can make anything, that "repent and be baptized," are in order to "remission of sins," the object.

Winer, in his Grammar, page 181, says: "Every case, as such, stands in a necessary connection, according to its nature, with the structure of the sentence in which it occurs." And again, he says, page 358: "The prepositions correspond to the cases; hence each, according to its signification, is connected with a particular case; viz., with that case whose primary meaning accords with the primary meaning of the preposition." That is, a given *case* marks a definite relation, according to its nature, in a given sentence. The preposition of *this case* takes the place of the case; or, it is employed in addition to the case for the purpose of greater definiteness or emphasis.

"Aphesin"—remission—is in the accusative case, which is the objective case, in English. The relation of, "repent and be baptized," on the one hand, and remission of sins, on the other, is expressed by the preposition *eis.* If the connection which *eis* makes in this passage is between "repent and be baptized," and "remission of sins," then and therefore, the repentance and the baptism are, and were declared by the Spirit of God to be for, or in order to, remission of sins.

To decide the question: What does *eis* connect in Acts 2:38, is of paramount importance in this investigation. We may safely refer the question for decision to the "ex cathedra" statements of scholars of all religious denominations, and of none.

1. First in this list, in some respects, I cite the name of the late amiable, scholarly, pious Albert Barnes, a Presbyterian commentator of Philadelphia. In answer to a letter written him by Brother J. B. Briney, he says:

"PHILADELPHIA, *August* i8, 1870.

128

"Rev. J. B. Briney:

"My Dear Sir—I received your favor this morning. My knowledge of Greek is very imperfect, and no great value should be attached to my opinion on a question of Greek criticism. But it seems to me the word *eis,* in the passage referred to (Acts 2:38), relates to the *entire previous sentence,* 'Repent, and be baptized, every one of you, in the name of Jesus Christ '—*eis*—unto, or *in order to,* or *with reference to*—the remission of sins, etc. That is, the repentance and baptism *both* have reference to the remission of sins; or the *entire process,* so to speak, in the Divine arrangement for the remission of sins, embraces this, or this is the *complete* process appointed by God *in connection with* the pardon of sins. Whether a man can be saved *without* baptism is a question not connected with the exegesis of the passage; but the design of Peter, as I understand it, is to state what *is* the *complete Divine* arrangement in order to the forgiveness of sins. (Compare Mark 16:16.)

"I regret that I have not a copy of the Syriac Bible, to answer your other question. I sold my library, and of the few books that I have I have no Syriac books among them.

"I am, very truly, yours, ALBERT BARNES."

Mr. Barnes here says that he understands the design of the apostle Peter "is to state what *is* the *complete* Divine arrangement in order to the forgiveness of sins." This is certainly correct. Then he says that "the repentance and baptism, *both,* have reference to the remission of sins." This is candid and scholarly talking by one of the truest and wisest men of our times.

Dr. Hackett, a distinguished translator and author, on page 69 of his commentary on Acts of Apostles, 2:38, says:

"eis aphesin ham action, In order to the forgiveness of sins (Matt. 24:28; Luke 3:3); we connect, naturally, with both the preceding verbs. This clause states the motive

or object which should induce them to repent and be baptized. It enforces the entire exhortation, not one part of it to the exclusion of the other."

Dr. Hackett was a Baptist, but here, at least, he writes simply as a scholar.

Lange's commentary on Acts, page 53, says:

> "This, *aphesis* hamartion, is, unquestionably, connected more intimately and directly than the gift of the Holy Ghost, with the baptismal act; the former, *(aphesis}* namely, is indicated by the word eis, *for* the remission, etc.], as the immediate purpose of baptism, and as the purpose inseparably connected with it, while general terms are all that now succeed, viz.: 'And ye shall receive the gift of the Holy Ghost,'" etc.

"History of the Christian Church," by Philip Schaff, D. D., page 61, says:

> "He, at the same time, called upon his hearers to repent and be baptized, in the name of Jesus, as the founder and head of the Heavenly Kingdom, that even they, though they had crucified the Lord of Glory, might receive forgiveness of sins and the gift of the Holy Ghost, whose wonderful workings they saw in the disciples."

Who Dr. Schaff is, no one, who is creditably well informed, needs to be told. The chairman, or president, of the committee on "Revision," in America, needs no introduction here. His language is so full and direct and conclusive, that nothing more can be desired. In the fewest and simplest terms possible he tells us what the apostle Peter said, and what he meant by what he said, viz.: that Peter exhorted them to repent and be baptized, that they "might receive forgiveness of sins, and the gift of the Holy Ghost."

"Theological Institutes," by Richard Watson, volume 2, page

624, says:

> "It is thus that we see how St. Peter preserves the correspondence between the act of Noah in preparing the ark, as an act of faith, by which he was justified, and the act of submitting to Christian baptism, which is also, obviously, an act of faith, in order to the remission of sins, or the obtaining a good conscience before God."

Watson was one of the most distinguished scholars and authors of the Methodist Church.

This extract is taken from his comment on I. Peter 3:21. I make the quotation here for the reason that if being baptized is "obviously an act of faith in order to the forgiveness of sins in I. Peter 3:21, it is, probably, the same thing in Acts 2:38.

In the year 1876, Robert T. Mathews, of the Main Street Christian Church, Lexington, Ky., himself a fine Greek scholar, addressed letters of enquiry to a number of the most distinguished Professors of Greek in our great institutions of learning, as follows:

> "Will you be so kind as to give me your translation of the preposition *eis* in Acts 2:38, and your opinion, as a Greek scholar, as to what grammatical relation it expresses between the predicates of the verse and the phrase, *aphesin hamartion?* I shall be obliged for your answer in the light of scholarship, aside from all theological applications of the verse."

Replies were received as follows:

Prof. Tyler, of Amherst College, Massachusetts:

> "Yours of the 9th inst. is just received. I shall translate Acts 2:38, literally thus: *Repent and let every one of you be baptized in (or on} the name of Jesus Christ unto remission of sins.* The preposition *eis* seems to denote the

object and end of the two verbs which precede in the imperative. In other words, remission of sins is the object and end (*or* result) of repentance and baptism. The meaning may, perhaps, be more definitely and unequivocally expressed thus: Repent and let every one of you be baptized *to the end* that your sins may be forgiven. The passage does not imply that repentance and baptism stand in the same moral, religious, essential or formal relation to forgiveness any more than believing and being baptized stand in the same relation to being saved in Mark 16:16, or being born of water and the Spirit, stand in the same relation to entering into the kingdom of God, in John 3:5. The result is fully realized in each of these cases only when both the outward and the inward conditions are fulfilled. But that the outward condition is less essential, is clearly indicated by its omission in the negative and condemnatory part of Mark 16:16, 'He that believeth not shall be damned.' I do not know that I have met the precise point and object of your inquiries. I have only touched the points of chief interest and importance as they present themselves to my own mind."

Prof. N. C. Cameron, of Princeton College, N. J.:

"The preposition *eis,* in Acts 2:38, is evidently used in its final sense, and the phrase is clearly connected with *metanoesate kai baptistheti* (repent and be baptized) as the end to which repentance and baptism in the name of Jesus, led. The conviction of sin in the crucifixion of Jesus, who was both Lord and Christ, led the multitude to enquire of the apostles, 'What shall we do?' 'Do,' for what purpose? Evidently, 'for the remission of sins, ' as shown in the answer of the apostle. They thought only of the sin against Christ, which, since his advent, as the essence of sin ('of sin because they believe not on me '); but the apostle makes the matter more general—'remission of sins. ' The term *aphesis* (remission), except in the quotation from Isaiah (Luke 4:18), has but one signification in the New Testament. This, then, was the object contemplated, both in the question and the answer, and to which *eis* points. Trusting that this hasty note, which does not enter into the question of baptism, or of its relation to salvation, or even of the meaning of the expression, *epi to onomati* ('in the name') is a sufficient answer to your question, I remain, yours truly."

Prof. Packard, of Yale College, Connecticut:

"Your letter of inquiry as to the meaning of *eis* in Acts 2:38, was handed to me this morning. I do not suppose it is possible to determine from classical or patristic usage a necessary meaning for such a word, which can be applied in any new case. It is so frequent a word, has so many various meanings, and expressing only relation, depends so entirely on the context for its determination, that each case must be decided mainly by itself. Here, it seems to be connected with both verbs. With *Baptizo* alone it has a special New Testament use, as to the meaning of which scholars are somewhat divided. My own impression (to give it for what it is worth) is that I should translate it, if these words occurred in Plato, for instance, *to the end* of remission of sins. It would then make *aphesin hamartion,* an object aimed at, or a result attained by the acts denoted by the verbs. But this leads one, necessarily, into the domain of theology. I am sorry I cannot give you a more definite answer."

Prof. Foster, of Colby University, Maine:

"Without a special examination of the passage in connection with others in which like expressions occur, I should say that the word here has the force of 'unto, ' 'in order to, ' 'for the sake of, ' indicating a result to be attained, and that it connects the phrase *aphesin hamartion* with both the foregoing imperative verbs, alike grammatically considered, though, on other grounds, I shall say, specially with the first, since pardon is nowhere offered on condition of baptism alone, while it is on that of repentance. This is, briefly, my response to your enquiry, as I understand it."

Prof. D'Ooge, of Ann Arbor University, Michigan:

"In reply to your inquiry, I would say that, in my judgment, the preposition, *eis,* in the verse referred to, expresses the relation of aim or end in view, answering the question, *eis ti* (for what?) and to be translated by 'unto,' 'in order to, ' 'for.' This sense of *eis,* as you doubtless know, is recognized by Liddell and Scott for classical, by Winer, for new Testament usage. I cannot agree with those who ascribe to *eis* nearly the same force in the phrase, 'baptize into the name,' but understand it then to be used in the sense of in reference to,' 'in relation to.'"

Prof. Flagg, of Cornell University, N. Y.:

"In answer to your inquiry about the force of the preposition, *eis,* in the passage of the New Testament, to which you refer (Acts 2:38), I should say that it denoted intention or purpose, 'with a view to,' much as if it had been written, 'so as to obtain remission of sins. ' I speak, however, wholly from the standpoint of classic Greek, not being familiar with the changes introduced by the Hellenistic. As to any theological bearings that the subject may have, I am wholly indifferent."

Prof. Proctor, of Dartmouth College, N. Y.:

"It is my opinion that *eis* is to be connected with both predicates, and that it denotes an object or end in view. I am inclined to think that the phrase, 'in the name of Christ,' though grammatically limiting only *baptistheti,* does, in thought, modify the connection of *eis,* the ideas standing, logically, in the following order, viz.: Having been shown your ill behavior against the Messiah, put faith in (the name of) Christ; on the basis of that faith, repent and (confess), be baptized, and then be for-given:—*eis,* connecting *aphesis,* not with the two predi-cates, separately, but with the whole preceding part of the sentence. I have, first and last, given a good deal of attention to this point, but cannot yet speak more confi-dently than I have done. If you enjoy this study as I do, I congratulate you most cordially. I establish few doc-trines, as such, but the Divine Word is, more and more, a sustenance and solace."

Prof. Harkness, of Brown University, Rhode Island:

> "In my opinion, *eis,* in Acts 2:38, denotes *purpose,* and may be rendered 'in order to,' or 'for the purpose of re-ceiving,' or, as in our English version, 'for.' *Eis ap he sin hamartion'* suggests the motive or object contemplated in the action of the two preceding verbs."

In these opinions from four great colleges and four universi-ties, in addition to what was said herein, before their introduc-tion, we have, for substance, all that can, or that need, be said on this passage. Authorities, of perhaps equal eminence, could be quoted to the same effect by hundreds. But really, the position held by these would not be made plainer or stronger by their in-troduction.

In the light of what is now offered, it seems to me to be the conclusion of a calm, unprejudiced one, that baptism is *"for,* or in order to, remission of sins."

The denial of this conclusion, by any considerable number of persons, is the unscholarly and illogical product of, compara-tively, very recent times. The great bulk of all learned and pious opinion of all parties in all ages, has been that, baptism is *for* re-mission of sins. Of course we are here, as everywhere and always, speaking *only of Christian baptism,* of the proper baptism of a person properly qualified to be baptized. God never contem-plated or provided for the baptism of any one not so qualified.

If the conclusion here submitted should be accepted, as it must be unless language be a cheat and a fraud; unless language be to conceal rather than to reveal ideas, it is a most pleasing thought that, 1. It is the deliverance of men infallibly guided by the Spirit of God into truth; and 2. It is in strict harmony, as we know it must be, with the great commission given to these inspired apostles on the eve of Jesus' ascension. In the commission we have the gospel that was to be preached and the commandments, promises, and threatenings, stated in words; here, we have the same things translated into *deeds* by the Holy Spirit, acting through the apostles. In the light of these facts and circumstances it seems to me to be nearly impossible to fail to understand correctly.

Acts 22:16. "And now why delay? arise and have thyself baptized and thy sins washed away, having called upon his name."

Here we have an account of the conversion of Saul of Tarsus. When on his way from Jerusalem to Damascus he was arrested and called, by the Lord Jesus, to account for his sinful and murderous course of life. Many years after his conversion, and when speaking as an apostle, he said of himself that he was at this time the chief of sinners. So, when Jesus began to speak to him, "in the way," he had not yet been pardoned. Jesus asked: "Why persecutes! thou me?" Saul replied: "Who are you, Lord?" And he said: "I am Jesus of Nazareth whom thou persecutest." Saul is at once satisfied that what he was hearing was true, and hence he enquired: "What shall I do, Lord?" Jesus replied: "Arise and go into Damascus; and there it shall be told thee of all the things which are appointed for thee to do." He went to Damascus, as ordered, and the Lord sent Ananias to him to tell him what was appointed for him to do. The first thing said to Saul was, "Receive thy sight. And in that very hour I looked upon him." Then Ananias delivered God's further message to Saul, saying that God had determined that he should know his will, that he should see him and hear a word or message from his mouth. Then he is commanded to "Arise and have himself baptized and his sins washed away," etc.

Up to this time Saul's sins had not been forgiven. True, he had heard and seen the Lord Jesus; he had been struck blind; something, as scales, had fallen from his eyes, yet he was a *sinner*. As yet there is no intimation or suggestion in the record that he had been pardoned, or that he thought he had received remission of sins. He was a believer, a penitent, and a praying man. He had asked what the Lord would have him to do and he was anxious to learn what his duty was and was *ready* to do it. The Lord had said to him that at Damascus it should be told him what he must do. He is now at Damascus, ready to hear and to do his duty. Ananias was sent to tell him what he must do, and his lesson is in the above quotation: "Arise and have thyself baptized and thy sins washed away." That his sins were not yet remitted is made certain by the language: "Arise" ... "and thy sins washed away." This baptism of Saul was, then, to "wash away thy sins." There are but two possible views of this language: one is that his baptism was for remission of his sins, *as a sinner;* the other is that it was for the remission of his sins, committed *after he became a Christian.* This latter view cannot be true. The scriptures do nowhere teach and no persons or parties in all the history of the Church have ever held, so far as I know, that baptism is for remission of the sins of persons which they committed after they had become Christians. This position being wholly untenable, the only other one which may be possibly conceived is: Baptism is for the remission of the sins of "*the sinner.*"

If this be so, then this passage is in harmony with the commission where, in reference to the sinner, it is said: "He that has believed and has been baptized shall be saved," or pardoned, and with Acts 2:38, where it is said to those who were already believers: "Repent, and let each one of you be baptized, on the name of Jesus Christ, for remission of sins." It is certain that Saul's sins were not *remitted before* his baptism. The language of this passage cannot be made to harmonize with the hypothesis that they were. After being baptized his past sins are not heard of against him anymore. That is, they were remitted when he was baptized.

The question: In what sense was he pardoned when he was baptized? is hardly important here, for he was not pardoned, in any sense, so far as the record shows, till he was baptized. The record shows that he was then forgiven. The record does not give the slightest intimation, even, that the sins of his, till then, past life were not then remitted, or that they ever came up against him after this.

In view of the, apparently at least, unequivocal and plain language of the verse, and of its treatment in the last few pages, baptism is shown to be for remission of sins.

Let us now see what, in part, the learned and pious have regarded as certainly the lesson of this passage, as it respects Christian baptism.

Lange, Acts 22:16, page 400–401:

> "Baptism a means of grace. It confers purification from sins, the forgiveness of sins. The invocation of the name of Jesus essentially belonged to it, as a confession of the Redeemer and a prayer for His atoning and justifying grace. *Apolousai tas hamartias sou.* Let thyself be baptized, and (thereby) wash off thy sins. Here, too, baptism is the medium through which the forgiveness of sins committed during the pre-Christian life is obtained. Comp. ch. 2:38, and I. Cor. 6: n." (Meyer, ad. ver. 16). Tr.]

Bloomfield on Acts 22:16:

"Anastas Baptisai. So supra 2:38. ' *Baptisthetd—eis aphesin hamartion,* reference being made, in each passage, to the method appointed by Christ for remitting the sins of those who *rightly* receive this sacrament."

Wesley on Acts 22:16:

"Baptism administered to real penitents is both a means and seal of pardon. Nor did God ordinarily in the primitive church bestow this on any, unless through these means."

Murdock, in his translation of this passage from the Syriac, says: "To be cleansed from thy sins."

Hackett, Com't. on Acts 22:16;

"Anastas stands opposed to *melleis,* i. e., *without delay;* see on 9, 18—. *Baptisai, be baptized,* or, with a stricter adherence to the form, *have thyself baptized* (De Wet.) One of the uses of the middle is to express an act which a person procures another to perform for him. ... This is the only instance in which the verb occurs in this voice, with reference to Christian baptism. In the analogous case (I. Cor. 10, 2) the reading is: *ebaptisanto* or *ebaptisthesan, Kai apolousai tas hamartias sou, and wash* (bathe) *away thy sins.* This clause states a result of the baptism in language derived from the nature of that ordinance. It answers to *eis uphesin hamartion* in 2:38, i. e., submit to the rite in order to be forgiven."

John Calvin, in "Christian Institutes," vol. 2, chap. 15. Ananias, therefore, only intended to say to Paul:

"That thou mayest be assured that thy sins are forgiven, be baptized. For, in baptism, the Lord promises remission of sins; receive this and be secure."

Calvin saw very plainly what we all see now, that if he presented baptism as "for remission of sins," men were liable to attach *to the water* of baptism, to the *baptist,* to the formulary of words used on the occasion or to the whole event, an undue importance, as though the virtue was in someone or more of these things. He took much pains to leave no ground for such mistake in anything which he wrote. In his great anxiety to keep the sinner's eye fixed upon the real ground of his forgiveness—the blood of Jesus—he sometimes used language which seems to be somewhat inconsistent with his general teaching on his theme. This he saw. He says:

> "It is not my design, however, to diminish the efficacy of baptism, but the substance and truth accompany the sign, as God works by external means."

Again he says:

> "For this analogy or similitude is a most certain rule of sacraments; that in corporeal things we Contemplate spiritual things just as if they were placed before our eyes, as it has pleased God to represent them to us by such figures: not that such blessings are bound or enclosed in the sacrament, or that it has the power to impart them to us; but only because it is a sign by which the Lord testifies his will, that he is determined to give us all these things; nor does it merely feed our eyes with a bare prospect of the symbols, but conducts us at the same time to the thing signified, and efficaciously accomplishes that which it represents."

In these extracts Calvin has used some words which we would not, now, employ to express what was clearly his meaning. At another place I shall have occasion to introduce this author again.

Chapter 4.
More Passages on Baptism

> "Or are ye ignorant that all we who were baptized into Christ Jesus were baptized into his death? We were buried therefore with him through baptism into death: that like as Christ was raised from the dead through the glory of the Father, so we also might walk in newness of life. For if we have become united with *him* by the likeness of his death, we shall be also *by the likeness* of his resurrection; knowing this, that our old man was crucified with *him,* that the body of sin might be done away, that so we should no longer be in bondage to sin; for he that hath died is justified from sin."

The reason for the language of the verses cited is found in the previous chapter.

Rom. 5:12, 13, Paul says: "On this account, as through one man sin entered into the world and through sin death, even in this way did it pass on to all men, because all sinned; for until law came sin was in the world, but sin is not reckoned when there is no law." (I quote from 'Two Fold.') Again, verses 20–21—"But law stepped in that trespass should be enhanced; where, however, sin was enhanced grace still more surpassed; that as sin had reigned by death, so grace, too, should reign through righteousness to everlasting life through Jesus Christ our Lord."

From this chapter, parts of which I have quoted, it appears that where there is no law there is no transgression, and, therefore, no sin; or, at least, there is no account made out against the evil doer. So, law entered to make men see themselves as they really were.

Paul's lesson is, that law was given that, in its light, men might see the real character of their conduct, and might know how to so change as to be in line with the will of God.

But, says the Apostle, "Where sin abounded grace abounded more exceedingly." Well, says a supposed disputant: "What shall we say, then?" "Is it the correct inference from this fact, that we should continue in sin that grace may abound?" Paul answered: "By no means." He then refers to the experience of the objector, saying: "We who died to sin, how shall we live any longer therein?" It was quite obvious enough that one who was dead to sin, could not, at the same time, be alive to it, or consistently live in it.

He, then, refers to the event and to the logic of their baptism in proof that one could not, consistently, commit sin nor live in it in order that grace might abound. He says: "Or, are you ignorant that all we who were baptized into Christ Jesus were baptized into his death?" The baptism brought them into the death of Jesus Christ. This he was supposed to know. Moreover, the apostle rather sharply reflects upon him for, apparently, not knowing this patent fact. So, if he had *died to sin* and had been baptized into Jesus' death, which had occurred for the very purpose of destroying sin (Heb. 9:26) it was clear that one ought not to suppose it to be right to sin that grace might abound. The apostle further says: "We were buried with him, therefore, through the baptism into the death, that like as Christ was raised from the dead through the glory of the Father, so we also might walk in newness of life." That is, the order of conversion was, people died to sin, were baptized into the death of Jesus Christ, in which case they were "buried with him," and, as he was raised up, having been raised up in a likeness of his resurrection, the baptized were, scripturally and logically expected to walk in newness of life. All of these facts, combined as the apostle combined them, made the conclusion irresistible that to commit or live in sin is not the way to make grace abound. This I suppose to be the lesson of this part of the Roman letter.

But it is manifest that Paul used some facts which were well known to his readers and were pertinent to his purpose in his argument, that have a decisive bearing on our main subject. For ex ample, he says they "died to sin." This signifies that they ceased from sinning, or from loving to sin, as one does who is literally dead. Then, being dead, he says, they were buried into the death of Christ, *in their baptism.* This signifies that, in their baptism, they were brought into the possession of the benefits or blessings to men, of his death. The baptized were *buried* and *raised up'* after a likeness of the literal burial and resurrection of Jesus, "to walk" (live) "in newness of life." With the rising up from their baptism they were logically, and we are now scripturally, expected and required to live new lives.

Let it be noted that the baptized were all buried *"with him"* were "baptized *into Jesus Christ,"* etc. Their baptism was, then, the event upon which, and the time *when* they came to be *"with him,"* (sun auto) when they came "to be *in Christ Jesus."* Paul says, in the 8th chapter, a part of this same argument, that there is "now no condemnation to them that are in Christ Jesus." That is, those in Christ Jesus are pardoned, but those out of him are not. Now, since baptism is the event that marks the *fact,* and the *time,* when one comes into Christ Jesus, it follows that IT is a condition of remission of sins; or, that it is for remission of sins.

Does one say: "But *before* their baptism *they died to sin."* Certainly they did. "Did they not *then* cease from sinning in fact, and also cease from loving to sin?" Of course they did. "Were they not *then* pardoned?" If ceasing to love and practice sin, or, having the heart changed, were the forgiveness of sins, or were it the God prescribed last condition of it, then, of course, when one's heart is changed he is forgiven. But, to be cured of the love and practice of sin is not to forgive sins, nor is it the final condition thereof. One may stop loving and practicing sin and still be a sinner. Though one in jail for murder should cease, *in his heart,* to be a murderer, yet he is guilty, the penalty still hangs over him and he must suffer the penalty of his sins unless he should be pardoned. It was shown in a former section that when the pardon of sin is spoken of in the Bible, the mere *love* or *practice* of sin, is never meant. It is the guilt and penalty of sin that may be and that are forgiven. When one has believed with all his heart on the Lord Jesus he has ceased to love sin, but he is not *then* a child of God a Christian. He, then, has the right, privilege, or power *to become* a child of God. So the word of God distinctly states. John 1:12, *et al.*

Verse fifth, of this chapter, is significant. In this verse the apostle says: "For, if we have become united with *him* by a likeness of his death we shall be also by ~ likeness of his resurrection, knowing this, that our old man was crucified with him that the body of sin might be done away, that so we should no longer be in bondage to sin."

We were told at verse four that our being baptized exhibits a likeness to HIS burial and resurrection. In *this verse* we are told that, in this likeness—in baptism—we are united with him, we are joined to him firmly, as though grown together with him. So, again, baptism seems to mark the time when we are, in fact, one with Christ, as we know that it, instrumentally, puts us into Jesus Christ. So, to me, the apostle seems plainly to teach. If this be so, then "Baptism is for remission of sins."

At verse 17, Paul, in answer to the question: "Shall we sin because we are not under law but under grace?" says: "But thanks be to God that whereas ye were servants of sin, ye became obedient from the heart to that form of teaching whereunto ye were delivered; and being made free from sin ye became servants of righteousness." In fact, the teachings that stood forth as a mould or pattern, into which the prepared people were put, or, as it were, cast, were: "How that Christ died for our sins according to the scriptures; and that he was buried; and that he hath been raised on the third day, according to the scriptures," etc. The effect of this teaching was to cause death to sin, or to change the heart. Then, those who had died were buried by or through baptism into the death of Jesus, and were raised up to walk in newness of life. Thus the converted re-enacted the whole gospel mould, in going through a likeness to it. Into this pattern of the teachings the people were put or delivered and were then made free from sin. Baptism was one of these teachings, was a part, at least, of the pattern of the teachings. And as one, then, was not made free from sin till he had obeyed from the heart the mould of the teachings into which he was delivered, it follows that baptism was for remission of sins, and that it is now "for remission of sins." I feel sure that the entire, splendid argument of this part of the great epistle is pointless if this view may not be accepted.

In "The Life and Epistles of St. Paul," by Conybeare and Howson, vol. 2, p. 169, note, it is said of verse four of this chapter, "This passage cannot be understood unless it be borne in mind that the primitive baptism was by immersion. Also, see vol. I., page 439." This passage, from so distinguished a source, I plead as a somewhat justification for the remark immediately before the quotation.

Gal. 3:26, 27: "For ye are all sons of God through the faith in Christ Jesus. For as many of you as were baptized into Christ did put on Christ."

The theme before the apostle's mind in this passage is: People become sons of God through "the faith in Christ Jesus, not by law." That is, I. In fact, we become sons of God *"in Christ Jesus,"* not out of him; and, 2. As to the mode of the fact, or the manner of becoming sons of God, he says: it is "through The Faith." The phrase: *The faith,* here signifies the gospel way of salvation, and there is no other way. There are a great many places in the New Testament where this phrase occurs in this sense. Then the apostle states the *time when* they became sons of God, saying: "For, as many of you as were baptized into Christ put on Christ." That is, they came into Christ when they were baptized; and they became sons of God when they came into Christ.

This apostle says, Eph. 1:7: "In whom we have our redemption, through his blood, the forgiveness of our sins." Again, Col. 1:14, he says: "In whom we have our redemption, the forgiveness of our sins." Whatever the phrase, *Christ J* may mean, it is true that remission of sins takes place "in Christ," not out of him, and that we come into Christ by baptism. If the statements of the Word of God are to be regarded as conclusive, as the end of all controversy, then the two conclusions, as above stated in the express words of God, are true. Now, as baptism is a condition of our being "in Christ Jesus," and as being in Christ Jesus is a condition of remission of sins, it follows that baptism is a condition of remission of sins, that is: Baptism is "for remission of sins." q. e. d.

Again, Jesus says that we are born of water, which is accomplished when we are baptized. See John 3:5. Of course no one is a son till he is born into the kingdom of God; and as no one is born of water, that is, is born into God's family till he is baptized, it follows that no one is a son of God, is in God's family, and that no one can inherit eternal life till he is baptized. If this be so, of course baptism is for remission of sins. But I prefer to tone down the sentiment of the last dozen or so lines to the following: I do not intend to be understood as saying that no one can possibly be saved unless he has been baptized. I assert only that the above is God's expressed way of the sinner's salvation. What God may do outside of what He has *said He will do,* I do not know. It is an impertinence to wish to know, if with the wish there goes a desire or purpose to try some other way. God has taught and expressed himself on the subject of the salvation of the sinner, on the theory that the sinner does not want nor need to know whether there is another way or not. A soul deeply and truly in love with God is not in search of another or easier way. He is certain to think that God has already given sinners the best and the easiest way possible.

Eph. 5:25, 26: "Husbands, love your wives, as Christ also loved the Church and gave himself up for it; that he might sanctify it, having cleansed it by the washing of water with the word," (or, having cleansed it by the laver of water, in a word—the gospel). *Hrema,* rendered in the new version, *"the word,"* and in some other versions, *"a word,* signifies: a word, a teaching, a discourse, an appointment or ordinance, a requirement or a gospel message. In this verse, the passage, *"to loutro tou hudatos en hremati"* I suppose refers to the bath or laver of water contemplated in the gospel where baptism is enjoined. The sense would, then, be that Christ cleansed the Church by means of the laver of water (baptism) provided for in the commission, which is Christ's *"hrema."*

That the laver mentioned here has reference to the baptismal laver will not, probably, be seriously denied or doubted. God's *hrema,* word, has no water in it except in the matter of baptism. Dr. Clark, Macknight, Wesley, Bengel, Stuart, the Methodist discipline(s), *et al.,* all say that there is here an allusion to baptism. Dean Alford says: "The laver of the (baptismal) water." There is but little difference of opinion among scholars on this point, I believe. This being settled, we are ready to enquire for the bearing of the passage on our subject.

After discussing the importance of living lives of purity and faithfulness to God, and after sundry specifications and illustrations, by means of which to make plain his lesson and to enforce it, he refers to the reciprocal duties and obligations of wives and husbands.

He says they stand related to each other very much as do Christ and the Church. He says: "The husband is the head of the wife as Christ also is the head of the Church." Again, "as the Church is subject to Christ, so let the wives also be to their husbands in everything." Then the apostle says: "Husbands, love your wives, even as Christ also loved the Church and gave himself up for it; having cleansed it by," etc.

Of this quotation, the distinguished and lamented Albert Barnes says: "In all this there is an allusion, doubtless, to the various methods of purifying and cleansing those who were about to be married and who were to be united to monarchs as their brides." ... "As such a virgin was to be purified and prepared for her husband by washing and by anointing, so the Church is to be prepared for Christ." There is this difference between the two cases. In the one case physical cleansing and purity are contemplated; whereas, in the other, the cleansing is from sin. The latter cleansing, the apostle says, as we have before seen, is accomplished "by the washing of water in a word." If one should be troubled over the manner in which the apostle puts his argument, it is not I that should be blamed. I am not attempting herein to suggest to the Lord how he *ought to.* put, and guard, and explain, his argument, but only, if possible, to learn and set forth what God has said. Now, if this "laver of water" alludes to baptism, as it certainly does; and if the cleansing from sin was by means of the laver of water, as the text says it was, *no matter in what sense,* it follows that baptism was, and, therefore, now is, for remission of sins.

Titus 3:4–5:

"But, when the kindness of God,, our Savior, and his love towards man, appeared, not by works *done* in righteousness, which we did ourselves, but according to his mercy he saved us, through the washing of regeneration and renewing of the Holy Spirit, which he poured out upon us richly through Jesus Christ our Savior."

The apostle, in this connection, in discussing or mentioning a number of questions, has occasion to refer to the fact that he and Titus and their Christian brethren at that time, had been foolish, worldly, deceitful, wicked, etc. He then gives some account of the fact that they were saved, and how they had been saved. In regard to the second point—*how* they had been saved—he says: 1. It was "not by works *done* in righteousness, which we did ourselves;" 2. "but according to his mercy he saved us through *the* washing of regeneration and renewing of the Holy Ghost."

"Dia loutron paliggenesias,"—through the, or *a,* washing of regeneration. What is the meaning of this language? No attempt'at explaining it must *contradict* what the apostle *says.* He says that they were saved through certain named conditions. This must not be contradicted by one in his attempt to explain the language. Explanation and contradiction are not compatible terms. *"Loutrou"* is one of the conditions *through which,* Paul says, they had been saved. Not that the *loutrou* saved them, but that they were saved *through* it, is what the apostle affirms. As they had been saved through it they were not saved without it. So, it was for their salvation.

This word signifies: bath, a washing, and, used metonymically, it signifies the water used in bathing and also the vessel containing the water. That it *refers* to baptism is the almost universal opinion of scholars. To this effect I cite a few authors. The distinguished Alford says: *"loutrou, pal.,* the laver (Eph. 5:6, note) of (belonging to, setting forth) regeneration, *i. e.,* the font representing the external portion of the sacrament of baptism and pledging the internal," etc.

Barnes says: "The word properly means, *a bath;* then water for bathing; then the act of bathing, washing, ablution. *Passow* and *Robinson.* ... The word here does not mean *laver,* or the vessel for washing in, which would be expressed by *louter,* and this word cannot be properly applied to the baptismal font. The word in itself would naturally be understood as referring to baptism."

Bloomfield, in loco, says: *"dia loutrou pal.* Render by the laver of regeneration. The ancient expositors almost universally (see Chrys. i, 323), and all the most eminent modern commentators are agreed that by *paligg.,* is meant baptismal regeneration."

Edward Robinson, Lex., says: "Loutron, *a bath,* place for bathing. ... In New Testament, *a washing, ablution, i. e.,* the act, spoken of baptism, Eph. 5:26, Tit. 3:5." To these, if more names were needed, might be added nearly all respectable commentators, ancient and modern. "Loutrou," I shall now, as I may reasonably *assume,* refers to Christian baptism in this verse. For some reason the apostle took care to say that the *loutron,* bath, in this case, was not just any *bath* that had been or might be practiced, but that it was the *bath-of regeneration,* or of the new birth. Jesus refers to it under the figure of a birth of water. John 3:5.

This bath is, therefore, not an ordinary one. It is *not the regeneration* itself, but it is the *bath,* or the *washing* that belongs to it. This bath, or washing, is the baptism of the great commission, where it is said: "The one, having believed and having been baptized, shall be saved."

Paul, as we have shown, says in this place that God saved them through this washing of regeneration, which is baptism. Therefore, "baptism is for remission of sins." The sense in which this is true is not the question before us now. This point is fully considered in another chapter of this work.

Chapter 5.
1. Peter 3:18–22:

> "Because even Christ suffered, once, for sins, a righteous one for unrighteous ones that he might bring us to God, having been put to death in the flesh but made alive in the spirit, in which he went forth and preached also to imprisoned spirits, disobedient at a time when the long suffering of God waited, in the 'days of Noah, while an ark was being prepared, in which a few, that is, eight persons, were brought safe, through water, which—the antitype, baptism—now also saves you, not a putting away of filth of flesh, but the asking of a good conscience after God—through the resurrection of Jesus Christ, who is by the right hand of God, having gone into heaven; angels and authorities and powers being put under him."

Peter, in this epistle, has, as I suppose, for his main purpose the helping of the dispersed to endure hardness—persecution—as good soldiers of Jesus Christ. He assures them that if they should maintain their integrity and faithfulness to God, though they should suffer, even death, God would reward them abundantly. If they should plead their innocence and purity of life in evidence that they ought not to be persecuted, the apostle would agree with them. But the fact of their suffering is not to be taken as proof of sins or crimes committed by them, nor as an unexpected or unprecedented thing. He reminds them that even their Savior, innocent and pure as he was, suffered death at the hands of just such wicked men as were then afflicting them. He cites the case of the wicked antedeluvians and Noah. He says, as an illustration of God's great desire to save even the wicked, of his being willing to suffer long on their account, of his merciful kindness towards them and the certainty that God would, in the end, destroy the wicked and save the good, that Jesus, by his spirit, went and preached to them through Noah, but that they did not repent. He says that God, after long suffering and patient waiting, used water as a means of destroying the wicked ones, and of delivering righteous Noah and family from a wicked, persecuting people, into a new world, cleansed from sin, in which they should live righteous lives. Peter says, the water which was used of God as a means of carrying those disposed for salvation over from the old world into the new, and of destroying the wicked, was a type of baptism—the antitype; and that the antitype, even baptism— now saves "you." This I suppose to be the real meaning of the passage. The apostle says that water—the antitype, baptism— "now saves you." Observe, it is not said that Noah and his family were saved *by water,* nor in water, nor from water; but they were saved through water as the mode through which God exerted His saving power. So it is in regard to the water of baptism, the antitype. It now saves us, *not as a Savior,* but as a mode or medium through which God exerts His saving power. To this God has tied us, though he may not have tied himself.

It is not an explanation of this scripture which says that baptism does not now save us, but it is a contradiction of it. I am aware that there is some difference of opinion in regard to the correct reading of the Greek text at this place among scholars. I have construed the passage according to the most approved Greek text.. But, so far as our contention at this point is concerned, no Greek reading claimed by any scholar would change the sense materially, I believe.

But it is sometimes contended that Peter does certainly say, that baptism is in this verse expressly said to be, not for putting away the filth of the flesh—sins. If the words, "filth of flesh," mean sins, the objection is valid. The Greek is: *"ou sarkos apothesis hrupou. Rupos* does not occur in New Testament Greek except at this place. Robinson's New Testament Greek Lexicon says it signifies, *"filth, filthiness."* Classical Lexicons take the same view. Sophocles' Lexicon of the Greek language for a period, from B. C. 146 to A. D. 1100, does not contain the word; but cognate words are defined as above. There is an allusion to the idea of sin in his definitions. Rev. 22:11, cited to prove that *hrupos* means sin, does not have the word. A kindred word, *hruparos*—is employed, and it is by no means certain, or even probable, that it is here employed in the sense of sin. John says here that the *"adikon* (unrighteous, sinful) shall be unrighteous still, and the filthy—*hruparos*—let him be filthy still," etc. I see no sufficient reason to think that *ruparos,* in this passage, signifies sinful. The unrighteous—the sinful—are designated in this verse by the term, *adikon,* and *ruparos* seems to introduce another class of persons. Be this as it may, and there is room for a difference of opinion, it is admitted that this word, not in the scriptures but elsewhere, is used in the sense of moral impurity, sometimes. But the possibility of its having such a sense in the third of I. Peter is cut off by the genitive, *sarkos—of the flesh.* That is, the cleansing in this case is not a Jewish cleansing from carnal impurities, which, under the LAW, required the bathing of the whole body in water. Peter says that this antitype—baptism—is not that; it does not cleanse in that sense. It is not a carnal ordinance. Baptism is the act of one, having a good conscience, seeking or asking after God. The being baptized is the act of one *(eis The on),* on his way to God with the purpose of entering into His kingdom. See John 3:5; Gal. 3:27, *et al.*

But, it is said, This one, who, by the terms of the record, is required to have a good conscience, before his baptism, must be supposed to be pardoned before his baptism. That is, the having a good conscience implies the forgiveness of sins. The conclusion in this case does not follow from the premises. A good conscience not only may, but must antecede the remission of sins. Nor does the remission of sins follow immediately, nor, of necessity, at all, upon the possession of a good conscience. Paul lived in all good conscience for years, during all which time he was the greatest of sinners. The passage means that, one seeking after God, must do so, having, *in regard* to the act, a good conscience. If one should fail of having a good conscience, in being baptized, he is not therein baptized, he does not seek after God, nor does he please God. The act is that of a hypocrite; it is a sin. But, when one is convinced that he is a sinner and has come to love God, and therefore, to hate sin, and repents, that is, resolves to turn away from sinning and seek God's forgiveness and enter upon HIS service, with an honest, true purpose, or in "all good conscience, and is thus baptized, he is saved. In a sense, baptism does not save him, but God saves him through it. In this sense baptism also now saves us. It is not for carnal cleansing, but it is a step, a Divinely appointed step, in the progress of one having a good conscience making his way to God, or to God's kingdom. If it be, as it certainly is, a God appointed step, lying between the lost sinner and the kingdom of God, then it is a condition of remission of sins; or, it is "for remission of sins."

On this passage, I. Peter 3:21, John Wesley, in his notes, says: "The thing typified by the ark, even baptism, *now saveth us.* That is, through the water of baptism we are saved from the sin that overwhelms the world as a flood."

The late lamented Albert Barnes says: "The antecedent to the relative, whichever word is used, is clearly not *the ark,* but *water,* and the idea is, that as Noah was saved by water, so there is a sense in which water is made instrumental in our salvation. The mention of *water* in the case of Noah in connection with *his* being saved, by an obvious association, suggested to the mind of the apostle the use of *water* in our salvation, and hence led him to make the remark about the connection of baptism with our salvation. ... The meaning here is, that *baptism corresponded to,* or *had a resemblance to,* the water by which Noah was saved; or, that there was a use of water in the one case which corresponded in some respects to the water that was used in the other, to-wit: *in effecting salvation."*

Bloomfield says: "The meaning, therefore, is that baptism, in order to save us, must not be the mere outward act, but must be also accompanied with the inward grace; in other words, it must be that baptism which our Lord described as the being born again of water and of the Spirit." See John 3:5.

Dr. Watson says: "It is also, obviously, an act of faith in order to remission of sins."

Bengel says: "Baptism now saves us."

Murdock says: We are "made alive by baptism. "

Alford says:

> *"eis en,* by having entered into which, [psuchai.] Acts 27:37. di'hud., by water bearing up the ark. [21.] Which (water generally) the antitype (of that) *(i.e.,* the corresponding particular in both cases) is now saving you also, even baptism."

Here I close my citations of the scriptures supposed to be in point in this investigation. There are a few other passages of the "Word of God," that might be quoted with good reason. But evidence of the correctness of my position would hardly be increased thereby. If it should be said that I have already quoted and commented upon too many scriptures; that if the position is really sustained by any one or two of the passages cited,

I then the balance of the citations were unnecessary, if not an impertinence, I should beg to say: The objection is, in one view, good. A proposition, proved, needs, for the mind that sees it that way, nothing more. But it is also true that of a number—a large number—of proofs which are separately, or ought to be, entirely conclusive of the proposition being considered, possibly only one of them seems to be so to the mind of A, whereas, other passages might strike the mind of B, C, or D, etc. with more force. This is, at least, the reason why I pursued the course that I have herein.

Section III.

Chapter 1.

WE have said, and repeated, that from the nature of the case, God only should be heard in deciding our question; for since he is the author of the decision, he only knows, in this sense, what it is. So called human authorities have frequently been cited, not because they have, of themselves, any right to speak, but because they are often of assistance in throwing light on various questions that have been or may be raised in regard to the teachings of the Bible. Their statements are of no force on the question: What must one do to be saved, except as they may, and they often do, throw light on the question: What does God *say* it is one's duty to do in order to be saved?

Again, where differences of opinion exist some persons may be much more apt to see or to know the right than are others. As a rule, all other things being equal, (i) Those nearest the scene are apter to understand its facts than are others.

Those who testify before any controversy has arisen in regard to a matter, are less liable to err than are those who speak after passions have been aroused by warm and even angry controversy. For both of these reasons those who lived immediately after the time of the apostles and of Jesus, would be more trustworthy in their statements on our subject, than are those of the present century.

I shall, therefore, conclude this examination by liberal citations from the most noteworthy writings of all the earlier centuries after the apostolic times, with a few quotations from those of more recent date.

Under the head, "THE CONNECTION BETWEEN BAPTISM AND THE REMISSION OF SINS," the learned and accomplished ex-president of Bethany College, West Virginia, W. K. Pendleton, says:

"In no age of the Church has she failed to assert the

obligation of baptism. So positive are the precepts of the scriptures on this subject, so demonstrative the practice of the apostles, and so unanimous the unbroken testimony of the great cloud of Patristic teachers, that no phase of evangelical ecclesiasticism has dared to so modify or change the uniform rule as to admit to the privileges of the Church any unbaptized applicant for recognition. Whatever else they may have differed about, on this point they have been a unit. They have said, with one voice: Between the world and the Church there stands the 'bath of regeneration.' Whether it be the Jordan, the 'much water' of Enon, the wayside pool on the 'way to Gaza,' the sculptured font of less ancient precedent, or the still later abridgment of the paltry pitcher—whether immersion, affusion, or rantism—in all time, through all changes, and by all evangelical branches, baptism, in name if not in fact, has been held up as the one indispensable 'sacrament,' without which the hand of fellowship could not be extended, nor the rights of citizenship allowed. Differ as they might about the 'doctrine' of baptism, they were unanimous in holding it to be a Divine requisition, and debate as they would about what is sophistically called the 'mode,' they had no controversy as to the duty of all to submit to it in some form.

If such be the place which this institution has held through all the centuries of Christianity, must not there be some reason for it, fixed and profound as the very foundations of our redemption? And what can such reason be, short of an established and recognized connection of some sort between baptism and the remission of sins? If baptism were an insignificant, a meaningless rite, a mere Oriental custom of apostolic times, a thing of fashion, or an accident of civilization, it would, doubtless, like the 'salutation' of the 'kiss,' or the courtesy of 'feet-washing, ' have long since dropped out of the fixed ordinances of the Church, and become a thing of indifference. On the contrary, not only has it been uncompromisingly maintained, but upon *grounds* which exalt it into a *significance* and *purpose* that justify the high importance which has ever been attached to it."

In speaking of the testimonies of "The Fathers," apostolic, the same writer says:

"One of the first distinctions to be made in studying their writings is that between their statement of *facts,* and their expression of their *opinions.* As to *facts,* their authority is certainly entitled to distinguished consideration; for they stood near to the things whereof they testify, and spoke under the critical and vigilant censorship of hosts of hostile commentators. True, they sometimes pervert the facts in order to fit them to their arguments; but, if we watch them as they are passed through the crucible of controversy, we can generally determine what is genuine and true. As to their interpretations of scripture, these were on many subjects, diverse and discordant. But where there is general or unbroken harmony, where there is no diversity, but the judgment is one and undisputed, linking itself directly to apostolic times, and passing down with unchallenged acceptance through all phases of controversy, and with every variety of theorist, then it rises to the dignity of a law, and though subject to revision under comparison with the supreme and infallible standard, claims a rank in our criteria of truth next to that of inspiration.

In introducing the Fathers, then, as throwing light upon our subject, we shall estimate their testimony by this rule.: Where there is unanimous, or almost unanimous, agreement among the great representative men of the primitive Church as to a fact or the interpretation of a passage of scripture, and this agreement can be traced back to an origin, if not in, at least the nearest to, the apostolic times, and without contradiction of history, or inconsistency with scripture, then we must accept it as of highest authority, next to inspiration itself, in our judgment and faith."

I.   I cite, of this class of writers, first, Barnabas. Who he was is not fully known. For a long time he was supposed to be the illustrious friend and companion of the apostle Paul. This claim is not now made for the writer of "The Epistle of Barnabas," by the best authority. This epistle is quoted as the work of the Barnabas of scripture, by such great names as Clement of Alexandria (seven times), by Origin (three times), by Eusebius and by Jerome. See Vol. I., page 167, Smith's Dictionary of the Bible. "The epistle is believed to have been written early in the second century." The date of the writing of this epistle is probably earlier, but certainly not later than 140 A. D. Barnabas was, probably, personally acquainted with some of the apostles and with their preaching. It is, undoubtedly, true that he was well acquainted with many of the disciples in many places, made by the apostles in person. So the testimony of Barnabas, whose epistle was read in the churches and was regarded as of almost equal authority with the writings of the apostles, is of the greatest weight.

I quote from the apostolic Fathers, Vol. I., page 120:

> "Let us further inquire whether the Lord took any care to foreshadow the water [of Bap.] and the cross. Concerning the water, indeed, it is written, in reference to the Israelites, that they should not receive that baptism which leads to the remission of sins, but should procure another for themselves."

The same, page 121:

> "This meaneth that we indeed descend into the water full of sins and defilement, but come up, bearing fruit in our heart, having the fear [of God] and trust in Jesus in our spirit."

2.   "The Pastor of Hermas." This Father was a contemporary

of Barnabas, with a probability of his having written a little earlier—say A. D. 120. T. and T. Clark, of Edinburgh, Scotland, editors
of the Ante-Nicene Library, say: "The Pastor of Hermas" was one
of the most popular books, if not the most popular book in the
Christian Church during the second, third, and fourth centuries.
It occupied a position analogous, in some respects, to that of
Bunyan's "Pilgrim's Progress," in modern times; and critics have
frequently compared the two works.

In ancient times two opinions prevailed in regard to the au-
thorship. The most widely spread was, that "The Pastor of Hermas" was the production of the Hermas mentioned in the Epistle
to the Romans. Origen states this opinion distinctly, and it is repeated by Eusebius and Jerome.

Those who believed the apostolic Hermas to be the author
necessarily esteemed the book very highly; and there was much
discussion as to whether it was inspired or not. The early writers
are of opinion that it was really inspired. Irenaeus speaks of it as
Scripture; Clemens Alexandrinus speaks of it as making its statements *divinely* and Origen, though a few of his expressions are
regarded, by some, as implying doubt, unquestionably gives it as
his opinion that it is 'divinely inspired.' Eusebius mentions that
differences of opinion prevailed in his day as to the inspiration of
the book, some opposing its claims and others maintaining its divine origin, especially because it formed an admirable introduction to the Christian faith. For this latter reason it was read pub-
licly, he tells us, in the Churches.

The only voice of antiquity decidedly opposed to the claim is
that of Tertullian. He designates it apocryphal, and rejects it with
scorn as favoring Anti-Montanistic opinions. Even *his* words, how
ever, show that it was regarded in many churches as scripture."
(Tertullian was a Montanist. W.)

It is admitted that there is some difference of opinion as to who this Hermas was. But his testimony is not at all affected by this fact. There is no difference of opinion as to the fact that these writings were held in the very highest esteem and even veneration by so great a personage as Irenaeus, who regarded them as "scripture." When we remember that Irenaeus was born, probably, as early as A. D. 160 or 165, and wrote towards the close of the second century, and that these writings had become so famous in his time, it is certain that they are very ancient and are entitled to the greatest weight.

This very ancient writer, who, though he may not possibly have been personally acquainted with any of the apostles, certainly knew many of their own converts, deposes on our question as follows: "Hear, then, why the tower is built upon the waters. It is because your life has been and will be saved by water." Hermas is here represented as conversing with a venerable lady from whom he gains all the information concerning the Church and salvation that he needed or desired. The water mentioned here through which he was saved is supposed to be the water of baptism, and it is not easy to see to what else reference could be made. See "Apostolic Fathers," page 335.

Again, on page 420, we read:

> "They were obliged, he said, to ascend through water in order that they might be made alive; for, unless they laid aside the deadness of their life, they could not in any other way enter into the kingdom of God. Accordingly, those also who fell asleep received the seal of the Son of God. For, he continued, before a man bears the name of the Son of God he is dead; but when he receives the seal he lays aside his deadness, and obtains life. The seal, then, is the water; they descend into the water dead, and they arise alive. And to them, accordingly, was this seal preached, and they made use of it that they might enter into the kingdom of God."

That there is, herein, an undoubted allusion to baptism is not questioned by any one so far as I am advised. I believe there is no room for doubting this fact. This point being conceded and indisputable, the lesson, as it respects our contention, is plain. "They were obliged to ascend through water in order that they might be made alive," is language that points to the necessity of baptism in order to life. Again, "descend into the water dead, and they arise alive." Speaking of the seal [baptism] it is said: "They made use of it that they might enter into the kingdom of God." In the times of Hermas, then, it is established that baptism was regarded by him, at least, as for salvation, or remission of sins.

3.   Justin Martyr shall be heard next. He was "born in Flavia, Neapolis, a city of Samaria, the modern Nablous." His birth "may be fixed at about A. D. 114." He was a man of considerable learning, and he is regarded as having been a philosopher of no mean distinction.

After his conversion to Christianity he became a most zealous advocate of it. He traveled much and disseminated a knowledge of that religion which, to him, was the sum of all that was beautiful and blessed. He is said to have suffered martyrdom at Rome about A. D. 165.

In the first one of his celebrated Apologies, which was addressed to Emperor Antonius Pius, et. al., on page 59 of "Apostolic Fathers," under the head, "Christian Baptism," he says:

> "I will also relate the manner in which we dedicated ourselves to God when we had been made new through Christ; lest, if we omit this, we seem to be unfair in the explanation we are making. As many as are persuaded and believe that what we teach and say is true, and undertake to be able to live accordingly, are instructed to pray and to entreat God with fasting for the remission of their sins that are past, we praying and fasting with them. Then they are brought by us where there is water, and

are regenerated in the same manner in which we were ourselves regenerated. For, in the name of God, the Father and Lord of the Universe, and of our Savior Jesus Christ, and of the Holy Spirit, they then receive the washing with water. For Christ also said, Except ye be born again, ye shall not enter into the kingdom of heaven."

Again, on same page, he says:

"And for this (rite) we have learned from the apostles this reason. Since at our birth we were born without our own knowledge or choice, by our parents' coming together, and were brought up in bad habits and wicked training; in order that we may not remain the children of necessity and of ignorance, but may become the children of choice and knowledge, and may obtain in the water the remission of sins formerly committed, there is pronounced over him who chooses to be born again, and has repented of his sins, the name of God the Father and Lord of the Universe; he who leads to the laver the person that is to be washed, calling him by this name alone. ... And in the name of Jesus Christ who was crucified under Pontius Pilate, and in the name of the Holy Spirit, who, through the prophets, foretold all things about Jesus, he who is illuminated is washed."

Justin, in this quotation, as almost everywhere, uses highly figurative language. Still, the entire connection being considered, there is no doubt but that the words, "born again," the name of Father, Son and Holy Ghost, "pronounced over him," "leads to the laver the person that is to be washed," "and may obtain in the water the remission of sins formerly committed," etc., lead to and justify the conclusion that Justin believed and taught that baptism is for remission of sins.

To show how careful Justin was to know and to declare the truth; and to show how ample and reliable his means of information were, I quote from "Ancient Christianity Exemplified," by

Lyman Coleman, as follows:

> "At an advanced age he (Irenaeus), a disciple of Polycarp of Asia-Minor, and the disciple of John, says of Polycarp: 'I remember his discourses to the people concerning the conversations he had with John the Apostle and others who had seen the Lord; how he rehearsed their discourses, and what he heard them who were eye-witnesses of the Word of Life say of our Lord, and of his miracles and doctrine.' This proves that Polycarp had diligently inquired from those who could tell him, concerning our Lord and his doctrine. He had made himself master of whatever was to be known."

Thus Irenaeus states and Coleman comments.

Polycarp was Bishop of Smyrna, a city of Asia Minor. His date is probably about A. D. 150. Irenaeus was Bishop of Lyons, and wrote near the close of the second century. In Asia-Minor he was personally well acquainted with Polycarp.

> "In writing an address to Florinus, a false teacher with whom, in his youth, he had enjoyed the society of Polycarp, he says: 'These doctrines, the elders who preceded us, who associated also with the apostles, did not teach thee; for, while I was yet a boy, I saw thee in company with Polycarp, in Asia-Minor; for I bear in remembrance what happened then better than what happens now.'"

Now Justin lived and wrote, probably, fifty years before Irenaeus did; he was distinguished for his learning and zeal, and traveled much. He must, therefore, be presumed to have had the very best opportunities for knowing what was taught by the apostles, and was every-where believed and practiced by the Christians.

4.   Irenaeus, of whom I have spoken with sufficient fullness, for our present purpose in setting forth the relation of baptism to our becoming united to Christ, says:

"As the dry wheat cannot become one mass of dough and one loaf of bread without moisture, so neither can we all become one in Christ without the water which is from heaven. And as the parched earth cannot yield fruit unless it receive moisture, so neither can we who, at first, are but sapless wood, ever produce living fruit without the rain which is freely poured out from above; for, our bodies, through baptism, but our souls, through the Spirit, have obtained that communion with the imperishable essence." Book 3, chapter 17.

5. Tertullian, a very learned Latin author of Carthage, in Northern Africa, and a Presbyter of the Church, was born about A. D. 165 or 170, and wrote about the closing decade of the second century. He was a voluminous and a very vigorous writer. In his Treatise, "De Baptismo," in the writings of Tertullian, Vol. I., page 239, he says: *"Quomodo ct ipsius baptismi carnalis actus, quod in aqua mergimur, spiritalis effectus, quod delictis liber amurf* which in English is: "As, of baptism itself there is a carnal act, in that we are immersed in water, there is a spiritual effect, that we are freed from sins."

Again, on page 231, Tertullian says: "Happy is the sacrament of our water (baptism. W.), in that, by washing away the sins of our early blindness, we are set free [and admitted], into eternal life." Again, Tertullian, Neander, Vol. I., page 646, Ecc. Hist., says: "When the soul attains to faith, and is transformed by the regeneration of water and the power from above, the covering of the old corruption having been removed, she beholds her whole light. She is received into the communion of the Holy Spirit; and the soul which unites itself with the Holy Spirit is followed by the body which is no longer the servant of the soul, hut becomes the servant of the Spirit."

But that Tertullian taught that baptism is for remission of sins is a fact so well known that no further citations are needed in proof. His very great fondness for the use of figurative language, which led him to indulge in strained comparisons and far-fetched or slight resemblances and analogies at times, leave the import of his language not quite clear. He seems, in some places, to ascribe to baptism itself magical, and even supernatural effects. The last quotation, however, seems to decidedly contradict this idea.

But it does not matter, as it respects our present examination, whether he did hold extreme views as to the efficacy of baptism or not. It is, at least, *beyond all doubt that the learned, sagacious Tertullian,* of the second century, who was, possibly, acquainted with some of the disciples of the apostles themselves, believed what, up to that time, no one, representative of our religion, ever denied, that "baptism is for remission of sins." Again, Tertullian says: "The divine grace, full and free forgiveness of sins, awaits those who will come to baptism; but we also must do what belongs to our part, in order to qualify us to receive it."

Again: Tertullian "De Baptismo," chapter 12, page 245: "When, however, the prescript is laid down that without baptism, salvation is attainable by none." See also Wall's History of Infant Baptism, in two volumes, Vol. I., page 55.

6. Clement of Alexandria was cotemporary with Tertullian. He was "the illustrious head of the Catechetical School at Alexandria at the close of the second century." ... "On embracing Christianity, he eagerly sought the instructions of its most eminent teachers; for this purpose traveling, extensively, over Greece, Italy, Egypt, Palestine, and other regions of the East. ... In the beginning of the reign of Caracalla, we find him at Jerusalem, even then a great resort of Christian, and especially clerical pilgrims. We also hear of him traveling to Antioch, furnished with a letter of recommendation by Alexander, Bishop of Jerusalem." Ante-Nicene Christian Library, Vol. IV. Clement of Alexandria, Vol. I.,

page u.

From these extracts it will be seen that his means for large and accurate information were exceedingly good. When it is also noted that before his conversion he was a distinguished pagan philosopher, and that, after his conversion, his character for fidelity and piety was among the very best, it will be allowed that his statements are deserving of much weight.

Of this Clement, President Pendleton says: "He was a man eminently spiritual in his views, and cannot be supposed to have unduly exaggerated the importance of baptism; yet, so strong was his conviction of the divinely appointed relation between baptism and the remission of sins, that we find him agreeing with Hermas in thinking that the 'Apostles performed, in hades, the rite of baptism on the pious souls of the Old Testament who had not been baptized.'"

Hermas' words are: "It was necessary for them to ascend by water, that they might be at rest; for they could not otherwise enter into the kingdom of God but by laying aside the mortality of their former life. They, therefore, being dead (or, though dead. W.), were, nevertheless, sealed with the seal [baptism] of the Son of God, and so entered into the kingdom of God."

Nean. Ecc. Hist. Vol. I., p. 646, corroborates this statement. He says: "Even in the spiritual Clement of Alexandria we may discern the influence of that outward and material conception of spiritual matters when he agrees with Hermas in thinking that the apostles performed in hades the rite of baptism on the pious souls of the Old Testament, who had not been baptized."

The name of the illustrious Origen is very familiar to all readers of Church History. He was born about 185 A. D., in Alexandria, Egypt. The time of his writing, or the beginning thereof, may be put at about 215. He was the pupil of the distinguished Clement of Alexandria. He wrote in Greek, and he was, probably, the most learned and the most noted writer of all the Church fathers of the first centuries of our era.

We know but little of what Origen wrote except as we obtain them through translations of them made by Rufinus and Jerome.

Rufinus says that the works of Origen which he translated had already been "corrupted in numerous places by heretics and malevolent persons." But another and greater source of doubt and confusion in the mind of one who reads what now purports to be the writings of Origen, is the fact that, so far as the translations of Rufinus are concerned, we are often at a loss to decide whether we are reading Origen, or only some additions, modifications, explanations, or glosses of the translator. In making his translations, he says, he "took care not to reproduce those expressions occurring in the works of Origen which are inconsistent with and opposed to each other."

"Wall on Infant Baptism," in two volumes, in Vol. I., page 67, says: "For, whereas Origen's books contained in them several expressions not consistent with the faith, in some points; St. Jerome changed nothing, but expressed everything as it was in the original, as he owns himself; but Rufinus altered or left out anything that he thought not orthodox. And in the 'Homilies on Leviticus ' he himself says that he took a greater liberty than ordinary." So, it is pretty well settled that, where Rufinus was the translator, we may not feel entirely certain that what we read is the real sentiment of Origen.

Moreover, though Origen was a very learned man, and probably, a very good man, yet he did hold a number of tenets which almost all fair minded men now regard as heretical. Still, it is not probable that one so learned and so widely informed, and, too, a sincere man, should be mistaken as to a mere *historical event,* which, if true, was a very notorious one, but if not true, was notoriously false. Such is the character of the subject matter on which we question Origen. There was no occasion that Origen should fail to give, on our present subject, an unbiased testimony; for, from the giving of the great commission by Jesus to his ambassadors, till Origen's day, there had never been a dissenting voice, so far as I know.

Again, Jerome (see "Wall on Infant Baptism," Vol. I., page 65), in translating Origen makes him say: "Having occasion given in this place, I will mention a thing that causes frequent enquiries among the brethren. "Infants (parvuli) are baptized for the forgiveness of sins." This statement is full and unequivocal. It needs no explanation. There are a number of other quotations that might be made equally as much to my purpose as this; but they are not all quite so well supported as the one I have here made. This quotation, if it be genuine, as it probably is, settles the question. Origen held that baptism is for remission of sins.

Whether Origen held to infant baptism, is not decided by this quotation. *"Parvuli"* the Latin word used by Origen's translator, does not necessarily, or even generally, signify infants, in the present current meaning of the term.

8. Cyprian, called by his biographer Pontius, "the devout priest and glorious witness (martyr) of God," was born about A. D. 200.

Not much is known of his early life. Pontius says of him: "Although the profuse fertility of his eloquence and of God's grace so expands itself in the exuberance and richness of his discourse, that he will probably never cease to speak, even to the end of the world; yet ... I have thought it well to prepare this brief and compendious narrative."

"That he was born of respectable parents, and that he was highly educated for the profession of a rhetorician," seem to be well settled facts.

He was converted to the Christian faith under the tuition of the Presbyter, Caecillius, at Carthage, Africa, in A. D. 246.

His great learning, genius, and perhaps, piety, sent him like a meteor along the line of promotion, so that within two years from the time of his conversion, he was ordained Bishop at Carthage, which position he held till his martyrdom, which occurred in the year 258.

In his letter "to the Clergy abiding at Rome," Ante-Nicene Library, Vol. VIII., and of the Writings of Cyprian, Vol. L, page 66, it is said: "For while the Lord has said that the nations are to be baptized in the name of the Father, and of the Son, and of the Holy Ghost, and their past sins are to be done away in baptism; this man, ignorant of the precept and of the law, commands peace to be granted and sins to be done away in the name of Paulus."

Again, p. 145, same volume, it is said: "'Alms do deliver from death,' and not, assuredly, from that death which once the blood of Christ extinguished, and from which the saving grace of baptism and of our Redeemer has delivered us, but from that which subsequently creeps in through sins."

In Vol. IL, page 185, in his "Testimonies, against the Jews," Cyprian says "that all sins are put away in baptism." See also, "Wall on Infant Baptism," in two volumes, Volume L, page 82.

These quotations are deemed sufficient to show that Cyprian taught that baptism is for remission of sins. They could be greatly extended if deemed necessary.

9. I find in "Neander's Church History," Volume II., page 665, *et al.*, quite a number of historical matters bearing on our subject, which I think best to quote verbatim from said author. He is considering several matters of difference then existing between prominent persons belonging to the Eastern and the Western Churches, so called. He says: "As it respects the doctrine concerning baptism, from which, for reasons stated under the

preceding period, the doctrine of regeneration was not severed, we must observe that the difference here again became strongly marked, which we discern in the views of the Eastern compared with those of the Western Church, with regard to human nature and the doctrine of redemption; namely, that in the Western Church, with original sin, the negative effect of the redemption in procuring deliverance from this; and in the Eastern Church, on the other hand, the positive effect of the redemption considered in the light of a new creation, were made especially prominent. Thus Gregory of Nanzianzus calls baptism a more divine exalted creation than the original formation of nature. Thus, too, Cyril of Jerusalem, addressing the candidate for baptism, says: 'If thou believest, thou not only obtainest the forgiveness of sins, but thou effectest also that which is above man. Thou obtainest as much of grace as thou canst hold.' This difference would be strongly marked, especially in the case of infant baptism. According to the North-African scheme of doctrine, which taught that all men were from their birth, in consequence of the guilt and sin transmitted from Adam, subjected to the same condemnation, that they bore within them the principles of all sin, deliverance from original sin and inherited guilt would be made particularly prominent in the case of infant baptism, as in the case of the baptism of adults; and this was favored by the ancient formula of baptism, which, however, originated in a period when infant baptism had as yet no existence, and had been afterwards applied, without alteration, to children, because men shrunk from undertaking to introduce any change in the consecrated formula established by apostolical authority, though Christians were by no means agreed as to the sense in which they applied the formula. Accordingly, says Gregory Nazianzen, to children baptism is a seal (a means of securing human nature in the germ, against all moral evil by the higher principle of life communicated to it); for adults it is, moreover, forgiveness of sin and restoration of the image degraded and lost by transgression."

Hence, he looks upon infant baptism as a consecration to the priestly dignity which is imparted to the child from the beginning, that so evil may gain no advantage over him. In a homily addressed to the Neophytes, Chrysostom specifies ten different effects of grace wrought in baptism; and then he complains of those who make the grace of baptism consist simply in the forgiveness of sins. True, the difference here becomes manifest between the more rhetorical Chrysostom and the systematic Augustin; for the latter would have referred those ten specifications to one fundamental conception, in which they might all be summed up together."

On page 666, same volume, Neander represents Isadore of Pelusium as holding that "Infants were not only delivered from the punishment of sin in baptism, but, moreover, had imparted to them a Divine regeneration, adoption, justification, fellowship with Christ."

On page 667, he represents *Theodore* as holding that "baptism, in the case of adults, has a twofold purpose—to bestow on them the forgiveness of sins, and to exalt them by fellowship with Christ to a participation in his freedom from sin," etc.

Same page, Neander says: "In this way we must understand what *Coelestius* says, in the Creed which he sent to Rome: 'Infants must, according to the rule of the Universal Church, and according to the declaration of the Gospel, he baptized in order to the forgiveness of sins.'"

In these quotations it is every-where manifest that these distinguished persons not only held that baptism is for remission of sins, but that they expressed views on the question before us quite in excess of what the Word of God authorizes or justifies. Indeed, it was, as early as the times of Tertullian, by *some* held that there was a Divine energy in the *water of baptism,* which was imparted to the one baptized, without regard to any preparation made for the ordinance, or any qualifications precedent thereto.

Tertullian, as we have before said, seemed, in some of his expressions, to have been under the influence of this error, to some extent. It is certain that, if not in the life-time of Tertullian, very soon thereafter, this error was a very common one. As early as the time of Cyprian, 252 A. D., this erroneous view of the magical effect of baptism was the common one.

The distinguished Lyman Coleman, in his "Ancient Christianity Exemplified," page 377, says:

> "From these Fathers we advance, omitting intermediate authorities of less importance, to Cyprian, in the middle of the third century. In the age of Cyprian there arose in Africa a question whether a child might be baptized *before the eighth day or not.* Fidus, a country bishop, referred the enquiry to a council of sixty-six bishops, convened under Cyprian, A. D. 253, for their opinion. To this enquiry they reply at length, delivering it as their unanimous opinion that baptism may, with propriety, be administered at any time *previous to* the *eighth day.* No question was raised on the point whether children ought to be baptized *at all* or not. 'This, therefore, was our opinion in the council, that we ought not to hinder any one from baptism and the grace of God. And this rule, as it holds for all, is, we think, more especially to be observed in reference to infants, even to those newly born.'"

See also, "Neander's Church History," Volume I., page 313, as follows:

> "But, when, now, on the one hand, the doctrine of the

corruption and guilt, cleaving to human nature in consequence of the first transgression, was reduced to a more
precise and systematic form, and on the other, from the
want of duly distinguishing between what is outward and
what is inward in baptism ... the error became more
firmly established, that without external baptism no one
could be delivered from that inherent guilt, could be
saved from the everlasting punishment that threatened
him, or raised to eternal life; and when the notion of a
magical influence, a charm connected with the sacra-
ments continually gained ground, the theory was finally
evolved of the *unconditional necessity of* infant baptism."

This Neander follows with an account of Fidus' question put
before Cyprian and his 65 bishops, so called, which I have already
noted. To put the argument into a few words, let it be said that
in the North African churches, especially in the time of Cyprian,
the prevalent opinion was that baptism was for remission of sin,
and by that time the opinion was general and de cided that "corruption and guilt," inhered in human nature in consequence of
the first transgression. Now, as *guilt* belonged to human nature,
it must, of course, belong to the infant; as the guilty one must be
lost if not pardoned, so, of course, the infant must be lost unless
it is pardoned. So they thought and reasoned. To meet this condition of things they determined to baptize the infant for remission of sins. Such confidence did Cyprian and his 65, so called,
bishops have that the infant was lost unless its sins or guilt should
be removed^ and so sure did they feel that to baptize the infant
was God's plan for its salvation, that it was the decision of 66
bishops of Northern Africa that the infant should be baptized as
soon as possible after its birth.

Also, they held that, "born of water," John 3:5, signified baptism; hence, they concluded that unless infants were baptized

they were lost. As to whether infants ought to be baptized or not, I have nothing to say here; I refer to the foregoing history to show what the opinion was in reference to the design of baptism and for no other purpose.

To show how intensely interested and determined they were, every-where, who accepted and practiced infant baptism, at this time and subsequently for centuries, I would remark that there were some embarrassments to be met and gotten over in the inauguration of the practice that required no small amount of skill to successfully encounter. It was the custom, in the Church, from the beginning to have the party about to be baptized to "confess with the mouth the Lord Jesus."

This confession the infant could not make. According to usage immemorial, the confession must be made else one could not be baptized; one must be baptized else he could not be saved. Therefore, as the infant could not confess, it must be lost unless some way of escape could be devised. To meet this difficulty it was determined that an *attorney* should be employed to speak for the infant. So, when the infant was asked: "(John F. Jones), do you believe?" etc., the sponsor replied: "I do." This absurd proceeding never could have obtained among intelligent people had it not been determined that the baptism of the infant was, at least, exceedingly important.

Gregory Nazianzen wrote during the latter part of the fourth century. This writer is so well known that no introduction is deemed necessary.

In an "Oration on Holy Baptism," Or. 40, § 2, Gregory says: "Religion teaches us that there are three sorts of generation or formation: that of our bodies; that of baptism; and that of the resurrection." Of the second—baptism—he says: "The second is of the day, and is free and powerful against lust, and takes away all that veil contracted in our birth and renews us to the supernal life." (< Wall on Infant Baptism," Vol. I., page 102.

Same volume, page 113. Dr. Wall summarizes as follows: "It appears most evidently by the tenor of this sermon that Nazianzen held, concerning baptism, these tenets: 1. That all who died unbaptized, by their own fault or negligence, were condemned. 2. He thought that infants dying unbaptized, and adult persons who missed of baptism by some unavoidable impediment, and not by their own fault, were in a kind of middle state between happiness and torment, but that baptized infants were partakers of the kingdom of Heaven.

Basil, latter part of the fourth century. Wall, Vol. I., page 132, in a sermon addressed to the Catechumens, "to persuade them to baptism," says: "and unless thou pass through the water thou wilt not be delivered from the cruel tyranny of the devil," etc. Again, on page 133, he says: "If a physician could undertake, by any art, to make you young again when you are old, you would earnestly long for that day in which your florid youth should be restored; and yet now, when it is told you that your soul, defiled with all manner of sin, may be renewed and born again by baptism, you slight so great a benefit." Again, same page, he says: "The sanctification of baptism you commend in words, but in your deeds you follow the things that yourself condemn."

Ambrose, Bishop of Milan A. D. 375, says, in a comment on Luke 1:17: "For that returning of the river waters backwards towards the springhead, which was caused by Elias when the river was divided (as the scripture says *Jordan was driven back)* signified the sacrament of the laver of salvation, which was afterwards to be instituted, by which those infants that are baptized are reformed back again from wickedness [or a wicked state] to the primitive state of their nature." "Wall," Vol. L, pages 138 and 139.

Again, on same page: "As Elias separated (or drove back) the waters of Jordan, so John brought persons to the baptism of salvation."

St. Chrysostom, born at Antioch, 347, was made Bishop of Constantinople A. D. 397. "Wall," Vol. L, page 143. After saying, in substance, that circumcision was a painful operation and did no good except "that by this sign they were known and distinguished from other nations," Chrysostom says: "But our circumcision, I mean the grace of baptism, gives cure without pain, and procures to us a thousand benefits, and fills us with the grace of the Spirit; and it has no determinate time as that had; but one that is in the very beginning of his age, or one that is in the middle of it, or one that is in his old age, may receive this circumcision made without hands. In which there is no trouble to be undergone, but to throw off the load of sins and receive pardon for all foregoing offenses."

Julian, in that "Homily," which he (Chrisostom) preached concerning baptized persons, says: "Blessed be God, who only does wonders, who has created and ordered all things; lo! they do enjoy the Serenity of Freedom, who but even now were held in captivity; they are become citizens of the Church, who were in the vagabond state of aliens; and they are entered into the lot of the righteous, who were under the confusion of sin. For they are not only free, but saints; nor saints only, but justified; and not only justified but sons; and not only sons, but heirs; not heirs only, but brothers of Christ; not only his brothers, but co-heirs; not co-heirs only, but members of him; not members only, but his temple; and not his temple only, but organs of his spirit; you see how many are the benefits of baptism. And yet some think that the heavenly grace consists only in forgiveness of sins," etc.

"Wall," Vol. I., pages 238, 239, quotes St. Austin, A. D. 410, as saying: "he never met with any Christian, either churchman or sectary; nor with any writer that owned the scriptures, who taught any other doctrine but that infants are baptized for pardon of sin." ... In discussing the meaning of I. Cor. 7:14: "For neither are unbelieving husbands or wives, how holy and just partners soever they have been, cleansed from the iniquity which keeps them from the kingdom of God, and brings them to damnation; nor are infants of how holy and just parents soever they came, pardoned the guilt of original sin, unless they (i.e., the one and the other) be baptized in Christ."

Again, page 245. "The carnal generation is liable to that one offense, and the condemnation thereof; but the spiritual regeneration takes away not only that one for which infants are baptized, but also those many which men, by wicked living, have added to that in which they are generated." Quotations, such as these, could be made from this voluminous author to a great extent, but the above is deemed sufficient to show what his position on our question was.

We have, incidentally, referred to Jerome's views of the design of baptism in former pages of this book; but I will now cite a few words directly from him. Jerome is here holding a dialogue, in which ATTICUS represents the Jerome side of the controversy, and *Critobulus* represents the Pelagian side. Speaking of infants, Atticus says: "These have neither power nor will, but they are free from all sin by the grace of God, which they receive in baptism." In answer to the question: "For what reason are infants baptized?" Atticus says: "That in baptism their sins may be forgiven." ... "But all persons are held obnoxious, either by their own or by their forefather, Adam's, sin. He that is an infant is, in baptism, loosed from the bond of his forefather; he that is of age to understand is by the blood of Christ freed, both from his own bond, and also from that which is derived from another." Again, Atticus says: "This one thing I will say, that this discourse may at last have an end; either you must set forth a new creed, and after the Father, the Son, and the Holy Ghost, baptize infants unto the kingdom of heaven; or else, if you acknowledge one baptism for infants and for grown persons, you must own that infants are to be baptized for forgiveness of sins; sins after the similitude of Adam's transgression."

Wall sums up, as follows:

> "The Pelagians confessed that adult persons were baptized for forgiveness of sins; but infants, having no sins, were baptized only for the kingdom of heaven. This was to establish two sorts of baptism; which was contrary to that article of the Constantinopolitan creed, then received in all the world: 'I acknowledge one baptism for the remission of sins.'" Vol. I., pp. 260–262.

Chapter 2.

THE foregoing citations of what are called authorities are deemed sufficient to show, to the entire satisfaction of the most interested and exacting critics, that all writers of note, of what party soever they may have been, orthodox or heterodox, held and asserted for the first four or five centuries, A. D., that the baptism of the Christian Scriptures was, and therefore now is, for remission of sins. During this period there was no dissent, no two opinions on our proposition. All who baptized at all, taught that baptism was for remission of sins.

If it should be contended, as in truth it may, that many of the ancient leaders in religious thought held very extravagant and erroneous views as to the efficacy of Christian baptism, we do not object. It is freely admitted that their views on this subject were, in many cases, wrong, sometimes foolish and even absurd. But this fact is of no force as an objection against our proposition; for, if I should assert that one is a drinker of intoxicants, and one should reply, saying: he is a regular drunkard, *a sot,* his reply has no force, logically, to show that my position is not true. The truth is, his proposition, proved, establishes mine also. This conclusion is based on the principle that the greater includes the less; that a man who is seven feet high is certainly six feet high. That is, if baptism is held by anyone to be for remission of sins and *much more,* he is bound to allow that it is for remission of sins, whatever else he may affirm.

I intended, when I began the preparation of this work, to quote in this connection from many more of the ancient authorities than I have herein. I purposed, also, to quote freely from the deliverances of many of the so-called Ecumenical Councils, and from the ancient creeds or symbols of faith. I purposed, also, to gather into this work the opinions of the more distinguished persons and parties of mediaeval and modern times on this subject.

But I have decided that further citations, however copious and pertinent they might be, would add no force to the testimonies already adduced. The case in hand is similar to one before Jesus once when he said: "If they hear not Moses and the prophets neither will they be persuaded though one rose from the dead." Therefore, I close my argument here.

Chapter 3.
Some Strange Things

QUESTIONS concerning our holy religion, both as it respects its faith and practice, have been dealt with, *strangely,* by many persons, good and pious, during all the centuries since Jesus was here in the flesh. So obscuring to intellectual perception is sin, that there are but few persons, if any, who have, on all questions, an unbeclouded vision of truth, even when it is fully, fairly, and affectionately presented. The same thing may, in truth, be said of us all when we are under the dominion of prejudice, though we may be unconscious of the fact. Therefore, we ought to be *slow* and *reluctant* to fault those who differ from us, or from whom we differ, however plain it may be to us that we are in the right and that the other one is in the wrong.

Notwithstanding these are facts, undeniable, it must be admitted, nevertheless, that we are permitted to believe firmly, and to assert with strong assurance of faith that certain things are or are not so. Though I have, in the preceding pages, at times, spoken confidently, and maybe, dogmatically, still, I have to the utmost tried to keep in mind, and heart, too, the thought that I am but dust in the sight of God; that I may be in the wrong and the other one may be in the right.

To be kindly affectioned towards his fellows is a source of much comfort to a soul. To take a hopeful happy view of the conduct of others is always a blessing to the one who does it. To be merciful in spirit; to rejoice, not in iniquity, but to rejoice in the truth; to bear all things, believe all things, hope all things, endure all things, are grounds of great, infinite, Divine blessings. Yet there is another side. It is not an act of piety to close one's eyes to a patent fact or truth. Nor is it a proof of one's having a wicked, perverse heart that he marks iniquity or error in another, and in frank, fraternal terms, on proper occasions, exposes it. That many persons have gone wrong in matters religious, is not to be doubted. That it is the *duty* of those who think so to say so, is a matter equally indisputable. That it is an *unpopular* thing to raise the curtain so as to expose to view the deformities and ugliness of the sinner in the church, is so well understood that the fact, simply stated, is enough. Therefore, not many persons are able to do the work of an evangelist—to reprove, rebuke, exhort, etc. Read chapter 23 of Jeremiah and learn how perverse God's people had become, at that time. Let it be noted that the mass of the people was not so much blamed as were the prophets and priests. These erred much and grievously in that they did not "speak my word faithfully, saith the Lord." This failure on the part of the prophets, to preach faithfully the word of the Lord, was the cause 01 the occasion of the people's going astray. Thus was the heavy hand of God laid upon the whole nation, but especially upon the false prophets. It has always been this way, and thus it is now—false teachers make God's people go astray.

Theoretic apostasy consists in departures in some sense or way, in *theory,* from God's word, and, therefore, from God. Practical apostasy consists in giving force and effect to a false theory by organizing on it and working to carry it out to its logical results. The term *Romanism* does not sum up all the apostasy, apostasies, and apostates in the world. Wherever the poison of unbelief "in departing from the living God," is found in the Church, there is theoretic apostasy. This may remain incipient and theoretic long, and it may possibly do no great harm, depending upon the nature and gravity of the errors in the case.

An error, no matter what it is, if it is held as a theory only, and while it is so held, giving rise to no practice or life, as it respects self or others, is perfectly harmless.

Departures from God are, in large measure, due to the fact

that those who read the living oracles do not approach the reading and study of THE BOOK in the spirit and with the gravity and carefulness that should characterize one who proposes to hold *personal communion with God,* while he reads and as he reads. Men and women may be found every-where who rack their brains and trouble their hearts much to ascertain where Cain got his wife. One who believes it to be wrong to pray, extempore, or that all right, acceptable prayers are *read,* is greatly troubled to know who held the candle for Jonah to read his prayers by while he was in the fish's belly. Again, one is greatly concerned to know what a "time, times and a half time," mean. He is so distressed that he cannot join the Church, since he is ignorant of the meaning of these strange words. Again, one is overwhelmed with em-barrassment as he contemplates the mysterious number 666. Such an one is frequently not lazy nor stingy. He will labor long and hard and spend money freely in order to understand the meaning of this strange number. The numerous precepts, com-mandments, promises, and threatenings of God, that are plain and on which is suspended the salvation of the soul, scarcely gain a nod of recognition from those honest, truth-loving souls.

Again, there are passages about the white stone, the bright and morning star, the millennium, Gog and Magog, the four beasts seen by John in heaven, the white horse, the black horse, the seven trumpets, the seven vials, the locusts, etc. Again, there is the man of sin, the son of perdition, the beast, and the false prophet, Babylon the great is fallen, is fallen. One enquires: What do these things mean? how perplexing they are, and who is "able for them?" Would it not be well if persons who are so troubled about the foregoing questions and their like would seek first the kingdom of God and His righteousness before giving any or much thought to these things which it might be pleasant and even prof-itable to a very small degree to understand, but a knowledge of which is by no means essential to salvation? These are strange things. Concerning no other matters do men act so without reason and against reason as they do in regard to the religion of Jesus Christ.

The class of persons who halt at and stumble over these, so called, troublesome obstructions, find no difficulty in believing stories, most absurd and ridiculous. I saw, in the "Apostolic Guide," of August 26, 1892, a quotation from "The Watchman," which is quite to my taste:

> "One of the surprises which constantly meets the student of Church History is the ease with which men can accept the most unreasonable and fantastic doctrines while rejecting the sober statements fortified by abundant evidence of the religion of the New Testament. The man who professes himself unable to accept the miracles of Christ will often be found to champion the most absurd accounts of spirit-rapping, mind cure, and theosophy. And frequently, one who professes to doubt the perfection of the character of our Lord will give the most implicit admiration to a fellow man or woman, whose personal life would not stand the test in an ordinary police court for ten minutes."

This quotation presents matters much as we see things around us every day every-where. Such characters are not peculiar to nineteenth century people. As now, they were every-where to be found in the times of Jesus on earth, and in the lands he visited. One would know of Jesus where he lived. Another asked if it was right to give tribute to Caesar. Another was very anxious to know whose wife, in the resurrection, a certain woman should be who had been married seven times. Some would learn why Jesus ate and drank just as did the common people; others asked why he ate with publicans and sinners. One would know what he must do to inherit eternal life, and was ready to do what might be required of him, provided his personal liberty was not to be infringed, he being the judge in the case. Verily, then as now, and always men were ready, willing, anxious, to be Jesus' disciples if they should be allowed to come in as they pleased and to live as they chose to live afterwards. This is strange.

Some of the fundamental conceptions of our holy religion are:

1. Man is a sinner.
2. He cannot save himself.
3. God, only, has power to forgive sins.
4. God, only, has the right to prescribe the conditions upon which He will forgive sins.
5. There are no means by which the sinner can know that he is forgiven except what God has said about it.
6. Therefore, one is or may be known to be forgiven if God says he is forgiven, but if God does not say so then we cannot, ought not to, must not, say so.

The theory that some are seeking to establish, that the sinner may know, on general principles, that he is pardoned, is hardly true. God has not left a matter of so grave importance to be inferred from general principles. Is one in the kingdom of God? Then he has been born of water and Spirit; or, he has believed and been baptized, for so the language signifies. Would one be saved? Let him believe and be baptized and he shall be saved. Or, has one believed and been baptized? he is saved; The one who has heard and has learned of the Father so that he is pricked to the heart and wishes to know what he must do to be saved (and no one else really wishes to know), is told to repent and be baptized. Thus plainly, definitely, does God speak on this point. There are no deductions of any sort to be made. After such talk from God, it is strange that one should wish to refine on statements made so plain in the word of God. Indeed, they are the words of God. Of course, the case is still more strange, of the one who, seeing these plain statements, should set them aside, should declare that the end that God offers *may be* gained, *must be* gained without the use of God's means appointed for that end. This is strange.

A gaunt, lean theory, to the effect that if one only believes he is saved, has a large currency among large bodies of denominational Christians, though it has no countenance whatever in the word of God. Again, it is claimed that if only the heart has experienced a strange impulse (and the more strange the better), which the one having it *thinks* is from God, and by which he *thinks* God meant to say to him that his sins were pardoned, then such one may rest in security, though God has not anywhere made the slightest allusion to such truth or fact. Is this not strange?

Does one say that to so insist on adhering, strictly, to what God says, and to so confidently rely upon the result following where one employs the God-appointed means, is, if not proof, at least suggestive of legalism? Well, it certainly is possible that one may become so infatuated with the idea of doing just what and all that God has required of him, that regard for the *outward* performance might trench upon the inner graces of faith and love, so far that his religion might seem to be, too, merely mechanical. Suppose, that in fact, we have a case of this kind before us, what ought we to do with it? Would it be right to insist upon less outward performance because the heart work had been somewhat neglected? Certainly not. Wherein one is in the right he should be approved and encouraged; wherein and to the extent he is wrong he should if possible be set right.

We have, in Matthew 23:23, and Luke 11:42, a lesson from Jesus' own lips on this point. He says: "Woe unto you Scribes and Pharisees, hypocrites ! for ye tithe mint and anise and cumin, and have left undone the weightier matters of the law, judgment, and mercy, and faith, but these ye ought to have done and not to have left the other undone."

I have read many sentences from the writings of some of the best men that, after all due allowances were made, seemed to say that the *outward* performance is not very important, if, indeed, it may not, with impunity, be omitted. But Jesus was himself an obedient servant, obedient even unto death. He was so punctilious in keeping all the law of God—in fulfilling all righteousness, that not one jot or tittle of the law of God was allowed to pass till all was fulfilled. Death, with him, was to be preferred before allowing even one, and that the least, of God's commandments to be disregarded or broken.

It has, no doubt, been observed, with pain and mortification, that, as a rule, when questions, as to whether given passages of our accepted scriptures are from heaven or not, have arisen, the class of persons readiest and certainest to decide *against* the Divinity of the said passage, is made up of, mostly, *young,* or of *comparatively* ignorant persons.

A reading that has stood the test of the world's scholarship for a long period of time may, it is true, be not entitled to a place in the Holy Book; still, it should not be rejected by the inexperienced or the incompetent unless a goodly number of *very scholarly* and *pious* persons have been forced, after long and careful consideration, to decide against it. In fact, it does not look well, and it is certainly not well to see and to allow persons, notoriously incompetent for such work, to cast out portions of what may be the word of God, on the slightest suspicion of their own, or on a mere hint from someone supposed to know or to be an authority in the case. Such persons make the impression on my mind that they are afraid to wait longer in making known to the world *their opinions,* lest they should not be thought to be, intellectually, in advance of the rest of the people. This, though not one of the seven or eight wonders of the world, is certainly and may be rightly marked a strange thing.

But of all the strange things talked of, written, or spoken of among religious people, I think, the strangest one is that a demand, even an earnest demand for a strict adherence to the word of God; that insistence upon a faithful "walking in all the commandments and ordinances of the Lord, blameless," should be looked upon by any soul that has tasted the good word of God and the powers of the world to come as evidence of legalism, or of sacramentarianism. Possibly, I should beg pardon for saying that I believe that the soul that in singleness of heart, that in deep love for Jesus, and that in faith and prayer yearns to *know all that* God would have it do, that strives with all its might to *do all* that God has called upon it to do, and that mourns in deepest sorrow when it finds that it has failed in respect to even *one* of the least of God's commandments, is very near to having attained to the best culture and the highest refinements pertaining to the kingdom of God. Legalism I Let it not be named in such connection.

And what sort of an *ism* is that which, like a hungry wolf on the scent of blood, is ever seeking a way to avoid rendering strict obedience to some of God's commandments and yet claiming to have the spirit of obedience? Such ones try to show that the will of God may as certainly be done by one who does not do his commandments as by one who does, with all of the probable advantages in favor of him who does not obey, but who has the spirit of obedience?

With such persons the point of greatest danger is not generally reached until these cheap sentimentalists reach the ordinance of baptism. This red rag in theology being reached, the worst possible symptoms of legalphobia set in at once and the subjects of it are filled with fearfulness and trembling. So, in some cases, at least, matters seem to me. My own opinion is that he who obeys God in the matter of doing *all* of his commandments, if possible, is as certainly spiritual as is the other, with a large preponderance of probability in his favor. Of course one may do the outward thing, and lack the spirit of obedience. In this we have the case of a hypocrite. His fault was not in doing *what* he did, but it was in his doing it *as* he did. But did it never occur to these super-spiritually minded brethren that we may as easily and as probably have a hypocrite among those who say they feel something as among those who do something, and that something a thing that God has expressly required us to do?

Hypocritical expressions as to one's feelings are surely as cheap and liable to occur as are hypocritical doings. The better view is, to "do His commandments," all of them, and be blessed: and this especially as God has said we must. The danger of our, thereby, not having or of our losing the Spirit of the Master is very small, indeed.

Again, one is wrestling with questions concerning God, and he refuses to be comforted because he cannot, fully, understand them. For example: God is said to be Omnipotent, Omniscient; is said to fill all space, so that he is every-where present as really and as fully as he is anywhere, at the same time. He does not fully understand these things, and he is not willing to accept the religion of the Christ until he does. So he talks.

Strange that such an one does not see that on his theory he should not eat, drink, walk, or talk. No one fully comprehends himself or anything else. He is full of mystery to himself. Much more must he fail, and *expect to fail* to fully understand all about God. Job 11:7. Zopharsays: "Canst thou, by searching, find out God? canst thou find out the Almighty unto perfection?"

The mysterious, the incomprehensible, confronts us at every

step, every-where, always. Not a spear of grass in our pathway, not a flower in our garden, not an atom or insect that floats in the breeze, not one thing, from molecule or the tiny life that spins its gossamer web in our window, to leviathan that plows the mighty deep, that does not challenge us with questions that are too much for our limited, poor, intellectual powers. We understand everything about nothing. Should this fact embarrass us? It should not, by any means. Nay, it is a most rational ground of real joy. It is a strong indication, if not a conclusive proof that there is a God and that he is every-where.

What one *fully* understands is certainly not God, nor a work of God. If everything that one sees, or of which he knows anything, were fully understood or comprehended, that fact would be proof reasonably satisfactory that no being above man was its author. Where the supernatural is not, there is lacking the evidence of God's being. The language of the supernatural is God.

He that acknowledges the existence of the supernatural must in reason admit that God is; for so the admitted fact signifies. The boast of being ignorant furnishes no way of escape for the boaster. Agnosticism is not an ism; it is nothing. But as it respects the existence of God, the things beneath us, above us, around us, and within us—all things—proclaim the hand that made us is Divine. That men will canvass the heavens and the earth; will spend and risk life and property to find, if possible, some evidence that all the things of human contemplation, visible and invisible, were always, or that they are here by chance, will, rather than to say as they were made to do: "There is a God the whole creation cries," fall back on the absurd negation: "I do not know; I am an agnostic," is strange. God did not make nor leave things in such shape that an intelligent man with fair opportunities could excuse himself on the plea of ignorance. Having all necessary facilities for knowing it is one's duty to know. He is not guiltless because he is ignorant; for, he has no excuse for being ignorant. That persons will so act with regard to a matter of so great importance, is strange.

A, somewhat, new view, and one not easy to satisfactorily discuss, is that baptism is in order to remission of sins; but that one's sins, or at least a part of them, are remitted when one believes, and also when one repents, as well. What causes this view to be difficult to treat, profitably, is the fact that it is not, or it has not been *distinctly outlined* by its advocates. Just precisely what the idea of the friends of this view is, seems to me not to be quite definitely stated.

One who propounds a theory is expected to present his subject so plainly that a fairly good thinker would not be apt to misunderstand him. A litigant is required, in filing his complaint in court, to so present his case that the point or points thereof shall be clear. A failure to do this is good cause for putting one out of court. If one has a good case it is assumed by the court that he can make a plain, clear statement of it. Therefore, a failure to make such statement is taken as sufficient evidence that such an one has not a good case.

If faith is in order to the *immediate* remission of sins, if repentance is for the *immediate* remission of sins, if confession or prayer is for the immediate remission of sins, and if baptism is for remission of the sins of an alien sinner, it seems to follow that the sins of such an one are forgiven in parcels. That is, a part of one's sins is forgiven when he believes, another part when he repents, etc. Is this theory true? I believe it is not. There is nothing analogous to it in reason nor in revelation. It is, however, advocated by men of undoubted ability and piety; so, though it appears absurd to me, yet the truth may be quite in its favor and I may be entirely in the wrong. It is certainly not said in the Bible, which is our only authority, that the alien sinner's sins are or ever were forgiven in parcels—here a little and there a little more—etc. If in this statement I am right then the theory itself is false.

Does the Bible teach directly or by necessary implication that one's sins—an alien's sins—are remitted, a part now, again another, etc.? I believe it does not. But do not the scriptures say, or imply, that faith is for remission of the sins of an alien? and that repentance is for remission also? I believe they do. In regard to faith read Luke 8:12, John 3:15, 16, 18, 36. In regard to repentance read Acts 11:18, 20, 21; 2:38; II. Cor. 7:10, *et al.* A careful study of these and other like passages in their connections will make it clear that both faith and repentance are for remission of sins.

If it were the intention of one to say, in Greek, that faith or repentance is for forgiveness of sins in the sense of its (either of them) being a step in that direction, or a move towards that end, with the implication that remission of sins is an end to be reached, he would employ the language found in the New Testament to express the idea that faith, etc., is for remission of sins. If this be true, and there is no doubt of it, then it does not follow that, where it is said that anything is a condition of remission of sins, we have proof therein that one's sins are actually remitted at the time or moment of his believing.

When it is said that the blood of Jesus Christ was shed for many *(eis aphesin hamartion)* for remission of sins, the expression does not *necessarily* signify that the sins of the "many" were to be remitted as soon as the blood was shed. Nay, it does not signify that the "many" or *any of them,* for whom the blood was shed, will certainly at once or ever receive remission of sins. The passage means that the shedding of the blood of the new covenant was, and is, as to its purpose, for remission of sins. Though the shedding of his blood was *(eis aphesin hamartion)* for remission of sins, or, in order to remission of sins of any given one, still just 'when such one's sins should be forgiven, and whether other conditions are or are not to be had, met, or complied with is not decided by this passage.

Eis does not, *necessarily,* bear the party who has the faith which is *(eis)* for salvation onto the point of remission, or into a state of the remission of sins. John 12:42, says: Many believed on him *(Qix.polloi episteusan eis atiton).* Here we have faith, which is in order to salvation or remission, followed by *eis,* literally signifying *into,* and yet the parties having the faith were not in HIM, they were not saved; for, they would not confess him because they were afraid of being put out of the synagogue, "because they loved the glory of men more than the glory of God." The fact is *eis* in Greek should i not *necessarily* or *always,* be represented by into, in English, though that is its current sense in the New Testament. It should, probably, in a few places, be represented, in English, by such words as *towards,* to, or in the direction of, etc. It is doubtful if *eis* is ever found with the idea of *into* or *whither* entirely absent from it. In a few cases it is probably impossible to discern the presence of the idea of *motion into* a place, condition, or state.

Mr. E. Robinson, in his Lexicon of the Greek New Testament, thinks that where the idea of *into seems* to be wholly lost from the preposition *eis,* as in a few cases of its occurrences, it is nevertheless expressed or implied in the connection. He says: "Sometimes *eis* c. accus. is found where the natural construction would seem to require en., c. dat. as after verbs which imply neither motion nor direction, but simply rest in a place or state. In such cases the idea of a previous coming into that place or state is either actually expressed, or is implied in the context." He then cites as authority for the position, Winer, Mathews, Buttman, etc.

It is at least certain, beyond the reach of respectable criticism, that where any certain thing, as faith, blood, repentance, baptism, or any other thing is said to be, *eis auton*—into him—or, *eis aphesin*—for or into remission—then that thing, whatever it may be, stands *between* the person or thing, not in the place or condition being considered, and being in said place or condition. To say otherwise would be to make the *statement* of the case contradict the real state of the case. That is, where it is said that faith, etc., is *eis* anything, it is in effect said that faith is *between* the having such thing and the not having of it.

The position, that an alien, when he has faith, and as soon as he has it, obtains remission of sins, and when he repents he again has a real experience of the remission of sins, and when he is baptized he has another real experience of the remission of sins, involves the conclusion that the forgiveness of the sins of an alien comes to him in parcels or installments. This conclusion is based on the false theory that where the Greek preposition *eis* is followed by remission, and is preceded by faith, etc., then we must believe that the remission, or a part of it, comes *immediately* upon the possession of the faith, and, therefore, before and without any other condition.

But the ground of this conclusion is not true. It often occurs, as to matters both temporal and spiritual, that one believes but goes no further, and hence he is not blessed. The step taken *towards* the blessing was essential to obtaining it, but if it is left by itself and while it is alone it is dead; it is of no value. If it be said that, *of course,* a dead faith is valueless, but that a warm, vital, or living faith has an immediate blessing in itself, I would say in reply, yes, but no faith is warm, vital, or living, while it is alone or until it proceeds to do "HIS commandments," to the utmost of one's ability.

There is, indeed, an immediate blessing for one having such faith as above mentioned, but it is not forgiveness of sins. It is the joy of a heart conscious of an intelligent, fixed purpose, having started, to walk on in the way of the life of God to the end. One who has so started out in the Divine Life, does, by faith, almost see the glories, the unfolding beauties and the sweet blessedness of eternal life at his very first step. Let no one suppose that I am here contemplating such an abortion of faith as is often had in meetings where numbers count for more than souls saved, and where the mode of success is a sort of whoop-up, hurrah, whip-in proceeding.

When I was a young man I was often absent from home and loved ones for years at a time. But, so soon as I resolved to visit them, and made the first step in that direction, my joys began. The joys were quite real, and very great, but they were joys born of *anticipation,* not of the *actual possession* of the grounds of said happiness. So it is when the lost sinner comes to believe that God is, and is a rewarder of them that seek after him; when he comes to obtain, through faith, a look at the love of God, the sufferings of Jesus for him; and when he comes to see the way open through the blood of the covenant to the joys of the endless life; and when he hears the sweet persuasions of Jesus: "come unto me and I will give you rest," when the sinner comes to see and to believe all this and determines to walk in all "his commandments," blameless, as far as he possibly can, he does not have to wait till he gets to Heaven in order to be happy. He is already happy. So I see things.

According to some misconceptions of some very good but misguided people, the happiness above mentioned is religion quite enough for them; they are pardoned they know, for they felt it. They know also that at the time when they had faith, only, they were forgiven.

The true theory is that faith is *(eis)* for salvation because it is a necessary step lying between the unbelieving sinner and salvation. When one has believed he has made a move *towards* salvation; and the move *towards* salvation had for its final objective point, "remission of sins," the being *"in him"* or "salvation." The same may be said of, or as to, repentance. When one is baptized the last move is made, the last step is taken that leads to the forgiveness of the alien sinner's sins. If this view is not precisely what the word of God provides for the case we consider, then it is, of course, wrong.

What we have herein said in regard to the topic in hand is written wholly in deference to the worthy authors thereof, not because I feel constrained to admit that it possesses real merit.

My purpose in these miscellaneous paragraphs, in the concluding pages of this work, is to specify and make prominent a few of the many strange ways in which people do act in regard to things religious and eternal. Of course, in the cases of those having such heads, hearts, and moods, it would be nearly impossible for them to see and to understand things spiritual, especially where the spiritual matters condemn the lives of the pretended learners, as they generally do.

In the cases of such persons, and their name is legion, the prophecy of Isaiah has fulfillment. Isaiah said: "By hearing ye shall hear and shall in nowise understand; and seeing ye shall see and shall in no wise perceive. For this people's heart is waxed gross, and their ears are dull of hearing, and their eyes they have closed."

The cause of this miserable state of the case, as it exists in our time, is not to be put to the discredit of the "rank and file" of church people so much as it is to that of the so-called ministry of the Church.

One is often compelled to turn away from hearing him who,

standing in the pulpit, claims to be God's messenger to show the people the way of life, feeling that, in view of the manner in which he deals with the people and with the truth, he cares but little for either.

Again, see how in haste some of us report, or induce someone to report every little thing done which is supposed to be creditable to us. And if someone should succeed in doing a right clever thing see how editors and correspondents proceed at once to glut the market with their eulogies of "the stylish and gifted preacher."

A specific remedy for this unlovely condition of things is not easy to find. I refer to this subject matter in general only to show how very difficult it is to make even a very plain point clear and acceptable to the average man.

The only remedy for this difficulty of seeing, hearing, feeling, etc., of which I am speaking is to, if possible, have those who are true, courageous and really spiritual to go forward and reprove, rebuke, and exhort to faithful performance of duty. Let the preacher who preaches himself and not the Lord Jesus Christ be told plainly, that except he repents he shall perish. Let the dose be well shaken when taken, and if a good result is not obtained, LET THE dose be repeated. If the patient does not improve under this regime, get a bad case of cholera or yellow fever and lay it close by the patient and give him another dose of God's infallible medicine and his foolishness will, probably, depart from him.